C000182490

In
Fen Country
Heaven

By the same author

Poetry
North Bank Night
A Man in Winter
The Dark Music
A Slant of Light
Last Train to Ely

Prose
Portrait of the Fen Country
Four Seasons in Three Countries
Call it a Summer Country (Summer Journeys Through the Fens)
Spirit of the Fens
Fen, Fire and Flood
The Solitary Landscape
A Right to Song: A Life of John Clare
Fen Boy First
The Winter Fens
Fen Country Christmas

Libretti
Katharine of Aragon (music by Barry Ferguson)
Old Scarlett (music by Trevor Hold)
No Cross, No Crown (music by David Twigg)

In
Fen Country
Heaven

EDWARD STOREY
Illustrated by Helen Hale

ROBERT HALE · LONDON

Copyright © Edward Storey 1996
First published in Great Britain 1996

ISBN 0 7090 5851 9

Robert Hale Limited
Clerkenwell House
Clerkenwell Green
London EC1R 0HT

The right of Edward Storey to be identified as
author of this work has been asserted by him
in accordance with the Copyright, Designs and
Patents Act 1988.

2 4 6 8 10 9 7 5 3 1

Photoset in North Wales by
Derek Doyle & Associates, Mold, Clwyd.
Printed in Great Britain by
St Edmundsbury Press Ltd, Bury St Edmunds, Suffolk.
Bound by WBC Book Manufacturers Limited,
Bridgend, Mid-Glamorgan.

For Renate Cave,
in memory of her husband
HUGH,
a truly great friend.

Contents

Acknowledgements

Once again I am greatly indebted to all those people who have willingly talked to me and have allowed me to quote from their conversations, letters and documents. In particular I would like to express my thanks to Mr Albert Bird, Miss Dian Blawer, Mrs Renate Cave, Mrs Constance Crouch, Mr Ross Davies, Mr Gordon Easton, Mr Roger Easton, Mrs Bridget Holmes, Mr Alwyn Johnson, Mrs Evelyn Merritt, Mrs G. Redhead, Mr Leslie Scott, the Reverend John Seaman, Mrs Cecily Weatherby (for permission to quote from the diary of John Peck), and to the Curator and Staff of Wisbech Museum.

The quotation from A.E. Housman's poem *Bredon Hill* is reproduced by permission of Random House UK Ltd; the quotation from Sir Peter Scott's autobiography *The Eye of the Wind* is reproduced by permission of Hodder Headline PLC; the quotation from Dorothy L. Sayers' *The Nine Tailors* is reproduced by permission of David Higham Associates; and the quotation from the poem *Poetic Justice* by Bill Turner is reproduced by permission of the author.

My thanks are also due to the editor of the *Spectator* who first published my poem 'That Place, Those Hours', reproduced in Chapter 11.

Finally, I express my appreciation of the help I received from my publishers and especially the artist Helen Hale who responded so imaginatively to my suggestions for illustrations.

Introduction

I had to ask myself the other day why I needed the Fens and why I have spent half a lifetime writing about them I am not a man of the soil in the generally accepted sense of that phrase. I have never worked on the land and have to confess that I do not even like gardening all that much. True, I come from genuine farm-labouring stock, especially on my mother's side of the family. For generations they had known nothing but landwork and all its vicissitudes. Although I always loved being in the fields, I knew that I never wanted to be part of the hard life they had to offer. I have since known enough farm-workers to appreciate the decision I made – if, indeed, I had any say in the matter.

Certainly when I left the local boys' school at fourteen my father asked me which I would prefer – to work on the land, or in the brickyards. Without hesitation I told him neither. I had vague thoughts of working in an office because I believed that it would not be as hard as being a manual worker. My father had never missed an opportunity of saying that anyone who had a white-collar job didn't know what hard work was. 'Well,' he said, 'the choice is yours. Now you've left school you'll have to earn your keep. We've done all we can for you.'

And so it was. Suddenly, childhood was over and although I had no qualifications for clerical work, other than a few months at a small commercial school where I learnt shorthand and typing, I eventually got a job in a solicitor's office in Peterborough and became a white-collar worker at twenty-two-and-sixpence a week, far removed from my family's roots. Or so I thought.

At the time, of course, I believed that the gates had opened for me on to a new and exciting world where

11

everything that a young man wanted in life was there for the taking. I joined youth clubs, music clubs, film clubs, and went out with girls who had been to grammar school. Surely this was freedom. Soon I was attending summer music schools in faraway Essex and believed that I had travelled almost as far as a man could go. My first journey on the London Underground was to be as awe-inspiring as any natural phenomenon.

Life now had both a rawness and sophistication about it that was stimulating and I found myself feeling sorry for those boys I had known at school who had gone to work on the land, in the brickyards or at local factories. At that time they were all rapidly becoming part of a past that I wanted to leave behind. They, in their turn, began to see me as a stranger and a bit of a show-off.

Such euphoria, on my part, could not last because in some loyal corner of my heart I knew that I had not been born to city life, or to crowds. I have always needed solitude and it was not long before I sought my own company in fields and lanes I had known since childhood. My eyes longed for distance, my awakening soul for space.

So, one of the answers I gave to that question I asked myself the other day, was that I needed the Fens as some men need islands, or as others need cities. They were to become for me more than a geographical area in which to exist. They were where I had to be in order to grow.

All landscapes have to be re-discovered and understood in the light of new experiences. The source has to be recognized and the roots found again to belong naturally in the ancient soil of some timeless existence. Sometimes we need to be exiled in order to find out where we do belong. It is only then that we realize how freely we enjoyed being part of a landscape, when we were not conscious of the influence it was having upon us and we expected nothing of it other than the daily pleasure it gave in making us aware of its presence. Later in life we may come to appreciate it more profoundly by knowing something of its history, but I doubt if that knowledge will ever surpass the undiluted joys we knew when the fields where we used to play were once our paradise. Even that word 'paradise' sounds old-fashioned now but, using it as the poets William Blake and Thomas Traherne did, I still feel it is the most appropriate word to describe the delights we knew as children when we could escape into a world of space and imagination beyond the narrow streets where the rest of our growing up took place. It can, of course, be a disastrous mistake to return to a place, or to a former time which we have held with some affection. There is usually a price to pay. We shall most likely be disappointed, disenchanted and probably made angry by what we find, for times change as well as places. And so do we. For some those past times can hold as much misery as joy, but not even they can forget. Why else are reunions so popular?

I think I first became aware of this need of a particular landscape when I was removed from it for a while to serve a brief period of National Service when I was eighteen. Until then I had experienced few other kinds of countryside, apart from those excursions into Norfolk when we went as a family for our annual holidays to Hunstanton, Cromer or Great Yarmouth before the war. My concept of the world was that it would all be like the Fens – flat, vast, full of light and flowing with bright fields of harvest. So it came as a shock to be sent to a training camp in the north of England. As I travelled by train through the grey, industrial Midlands and the mill towns of Lancashire, I could not believe that I was still in the same country. Seeing them so soon after the war they probably looked even more depressingly drab. It was not that my home town of Whittlesey was beautiful for, in those days, we were still surrounded by scores of towering brickyard chimneys constantly oozing out their heavy smoke and, although we had Gracious Street and Queen Street, the town had few houses to fit those definitions. As I progressed north, however, it was not long before I felt painfully homesick for the fields at home, for those wide, uncluttered spaces that I had known all my life. I longed for my first weeks of 'square-bashing' to pass so that I could earn my forty-eight-hour pass and hurry back to the Fens with their unregimented skies. I had never been away from them for so long.

The strange new world to which I had been sent was as alien to me as were the many dialects I now heard among the other recruits – boys from the Rhondda Valley,

Rochdale, Rotherham, Newcastle and Stepney. In such company I felt that my education was only just beginning. Most of those boys were far more worldly-wise than I. To begin with I was intrigued by the furtive dealings that went on behind the huts, some bartering cigarettes for dirty postcards, others planning break-ins to the cookhouse to steal extra food, some even whispering of escape. We slept twenty-four to a hut, and were shouted at all day by uncouth NCOs whose aim in life was to humiliate all those mothers' little darlings who had been snatched from the comforts of pampering home.

Each day the Fens and all they stood for seemed further away than ever and I soon realized that I did not belong to this anonymous, unfeeling world of fences and tarmac, but to a particular place. I hungered for its nourishment, its warmth, light and understanding. When I was at last allowed to go home for my first weekend leave I felt like a child on Christmas morning. The railway journey from Warrington to Rugby was the slow recovery from a nightmare. The next part of the journey from Rugby to Peterborough was the realization of a dream coming true. I began to smell the air of the Fens and I thrust my head out of the carriage window to breathe in more, almost losing my regimental cap as I did so. (In those days we had to wear uniform even going on leave.) Then, at last, the familiar, jolting bus ride from the city bus station to Whittlesey, with its now welcoming smells of the brickyards and the black peat soil of the fields beyond. I stayed in the house just long enough to have a cup of tea, telling the family something of the regime at camp and all my heroic deeds, then I changed into my sports-clothes already smelling of moth-balls, collected my bike from the shed, and rode out of the yard, down Ramsey Road towards Pondersbridge and shouted loudly for joy. There were the everlasting fields that I had missed so much. There was the country that I wanted to defend in my own way and for which I did not need a uniform, or a drill-sergeant yelling at me.

What I also knew then was that I had to learn more about those fields and the people who lived and worked on them. Their history was, at that time, virtually unknown to me. I had been selfish in my indulgence and perhaps too romantic in my affection for the place, taking it all for granted. One thing I had discovered during my six weeks in the RAF was that several of the other boys could tell me much more about their home towns than I knew about mine, especially those lads from the mining valleys of Yorkshire and South Wales. The pits were in their blood, even if they had not worked in them. It was the history and the traditions that made them proud. They were already conscious of what greed and industry could do to a landscape and its people. So what about my town? Where was the reality?

Fortunately, because a few of us did not measure up to the Services' idea of fitness we were discharged on medical grounds and I was allowed to go home sooner than expected. The prodigal son had returned. But that also presented something of a problem. At precisely the same time it became clear to my former employers that it was an appropriate moment for me and the legal profession to part company. I tried to make it sound like a mutual agreement for in those days there was an incurable stigma about being given the sack. Probably there still is, but now employees have the protection of industrial tribunals over unfair dismissals and a change of career can be seen as ambitious. No matter how hard I wriggled to describe my change of fortune, nothing could disguise its reality. I was out of a job. What was I to do now? It took time but eventually the Fens supplied the answer. There were a few experiments along the way – working in a music shop, for a garage, in a factory, for a potato-merchant, then back to an office – until I finally became a writer.

This book is a celebration of what these later years and this special landscape has done for me. When I told my friends what I was doing there was a chorus of 'Not another book about the Fens!' But I was able to reply, 'Don't worry, there is always something new to discover.' And, in the following chapters there are descriptions of places I had never been to before, interviews with people I did not know and some remarkable stories that I was hearing for the first time. There were, again, some most enjoyable encounters.

Now that the book is finished I am able to look back and see just how fortunate I was to be writing it in a year that was to be blessed with one of the best summers of this century, one that provided us with a bountiful harvest, and the warmest October since records began in 1659. Could I have asked for more? Not at the time. Nor would I expect any year to be more generous. But before allowing the following chapters to proclaim the many joys I received I must also sound a note of warning. Much has changed since I first began writing about this particular landscape, as it has in most of rural England. Despite all the efforts of those organizations trying to protect our countryside, a large part of what we believe we treasure is, nevertheless, disappearing before our very eyes. More roads, more traffic, more building development, more out-of-town supermarkets, more noise. Consequently we are more than ever in danger of letting this heaven slip from our grasp. Pollution, radioactive waste and neglect could make our earth a hell rather than the paradise we would like it to be. I wrote this book not only to praise but also to preserve something of what we might otherwise lose, forever. It may be that in time it will only remind us of what we have lost. If so, that will make it a sad and unintended epitaph.

I trust that what I have written will ring with optimism rather than pessimism. If nothing else I would like this book to stand as a token of my thanks to all those people who have shared with me this love of the Fens. Their lives are surely worthy of our gratitude. Their example something we could do worse than follow.

E.S. 1996

Part 1

Fine Fields and Fen People

Earth's crammed with heaven,
And every common bush afire with God;
But only he who sees, takes off his shoes;
The rest sit round and pluck blackberries.

Elizabeth Barrett Browning

1   Walking Where the Water was

I am often asked which is my favourite spot in the Fens, my own chosen piece of Fen country heaven. Apart from not always being prepared to divulge that secret, I have to say that it is an almost impossible question to answer. The favourite place will depend on the kind of day, the time of year and my mood. What I do know is that it must never be far away from water because, well-drained though the Fens are these days, water is still an integral part of the landscape. So rivers, dykes, meres and washlands have a special attraction for me. Then there are those wild, almost displaced areas between the farms and the sea, a kind of borrowed land that exists because man has tamed the waters. It is land which, as we know from experience, the sea could reclaim any time it stirred itself into a temper.

However, in a moment of magnanimity, I am prepared to admit that one of the best places where earth and water meet is along the shores of the Wash. This is where our three main fenland rivers – the Great Ouse, the Nene and the Welland – slither unceremoniously into another world. I have stood at this point of conflux on many occasions and each time it has been a different experience. In wintertime it can feel like the end of the world. In summer it feels more like the beginning of time.

For the purpose of this book I have chosen to write about a day spent there on what is now recorded as the hottest July of the century – July 1995. The weeks that followed were also to make it one of the driest summers of all time but we were not to know that on the day my wife and I set off early for Guy's Head, near Sutton Bridge, complete with a well-stocked picnic-basket and the dog.

The drive from Thorney to Sutton St Edmund, Tydd St Giles and Tydd Gote was a perfect prelude to the day. I am

certain that I have never seen so much wheat being grown
in one year. There were thousands of acres of it, burnished
and dry, just ready for harvesting. In the distance there
was still a slight haze waiting to be burnt off by the sun. A
group of pylons stood like monolithic chess-pieces poised
in an eternal checkmate.

We drove on to Sutton Bridge and Wingland. Still more
wheat – tall, firm, heavy-eared and already looking as
brown as newly baked bread. As soon as we had crossed
the lava-flow of traffic on the A17 and turned on to the
narrow Wingland road, we felt an instant transformation.
We knew that we were entering another world, a world of
space, water, mystery and sky. Along the artificial cut that
ends the River Nene's journey to the Wash, small boats
were moored, including the river pilot's. The scene was
now being set and for three miles we were happily lured
towards Guy's Head and the edge of man's territory.

It was at Guy's Head that Sir Peter Scott chose to settle
from 1933–9, in the then fairly primitive lighthouse. There
are two lighthouses, one on the west bank and one on the
east of the river. They serve no practical purpose as far as
shipping is concerned but were built to commemorate the
completion of the Nene Cut, which Dorothy L. Sayers was
to feature in her novel *The Nine Tailors*. This cut was part of
the final stages of the drainage operations that were
started in the Fens during the seventeenth and eighteenth
centuries – a splendid achievement then, considering it
was virtually all manual work, but mistakes were made
and subsequent engineers had to remedy them. If the
Fens were to be kept dry it was imperative that the inland
waters should flow into the Wash as smoothly as possible
and that the outfalls be prevented from silting up, causing
flooding.

I shall return to the story of Sir Peter Scott a little later
but first of all it is important to establish the nature of the
landscape itself for, by the time the lighthouse is reached,
one is already walking where the sea once was less than a
thousand years ago. In AD 1086 the Wash coastline would
have been much further inland, as much as nine miles at
some sections. The town of Wisbech was then an
important seaport. Holbeach, Long Sutton, Walsoken and
West Walton would have heard the tides lapping at their
parish boundaries. This is why there have been arguments

about where, precisely, King John lost his jewels (if he did) when crossing the Wash in 1215.

Now, between these habitations and the shoreline, it is possible to walk at any time of the year on land that has been won from the sea. It does not need a great imagination to hear voices in the wind, ghosts maybe of those mariners who never made landfall many centuries ago. But even that distant scene is relatively recent. After the last Ice Age the sea extended as much as thirty miles inland. Little wonder that there are times when this part of the Fens feels like a haunted kingdom.

We parked the car near the lighthouse and strolled towards the sea-wall. I stopped to have a few words with a man who came from Walpole St Andrew, a village two miles to the east. Naturally we spoke of the exceptionally warm weather. Then, trying to extend the conversation, I asked him what it was like out there in the winter. His keen blue eyes looked at me as if I had said something quite stupid. 'Winter? I've never bin out 'ere in the winter. Why would I want to do that?'

I caught up with my wife and we continued our planned walk. Several feet below us grew yet more wheat, as perfect as any farmer could wish, a vast, dried-out ocean with only one tide left. Walking towards Norfolk I began to imagine that I could hear more than the cries of drowning sailors or the low throb of a muddy sea receding. There was also the slow crack of some prehistoric ice-pack breaking as these islands of ours came into being, painfully severed from the main European continent ten thousand years before the politicians attempted to put them all back together again. There, too, was the groaning of the earth's crust crumbling under the weight of melting snow and the flooding of old land by virgin waters. This was where our history began, where the Fens were eventually brought into being and by which they still might meet their end. Even the black Fens of Cambridgeshire, created by the trapped waters that could not reach the sea, owe their existence to this early geological schism. This brooding land will always be a battleground and there are times when it feels as if one is standing on the precipice of the Dark Ages.

It was also over these waters that, a thousand years later, the Viking longships were to bring those sea-warriors who came to plunder the new great abbeys that had been established in East Anglia. Then flames and bloodshed were added to the terrors of the elements. But shorelines are not only places of arrival. They are also points of departure. Islanders always want to be explorers. Where would some of our famous travellers have been without a coastal path to walk, a rock to sit on or a jetty on which to dream of other worlds as the waves beckoned? As we stood there that late July day, it felt as if we were at both a beginning and an end, in a neutral zone that was not conditioned by time or distance. Space allows the mind to travel anywhere and there is always a tremendous sense of freedom along that sea-wall walk. It is where one learns again that the secret of contentment is to simplify, to shed the unnecessary backpack of material values, worries and trivia that can weigh us down.

Perhaps these were some of the qualities that persuaded Sir Peter Scott to spend those years out here in that uncertain period of history between two world wars. From his studio he could see the dawn break and watch the flight patterns of nearly a hundred different species of birds and wildfowl, from curlews, oystercatchers, dunlin and pintail, to redshank, shelduck, mallards, pink-footed geese and brent geese. In wintertime it is estimated that 180,000 birds will gather on the mudflats of the Wash. For the artist these birds were seen against a daily backdrop of sky that would have been different every time he set up his easel. Even in the thirties the water came in much closer than it does today. Modern land reclamation has pushed the Wash still further out and now it is only at high spring tides, or floods, that we get any idea of what it was really like before the sea yielded up more of its ancient territory.

Before Sir Peter Scott leased the lighthouse from the Nene Catchment Board for £5 a year, it was used occasionally as a hailing post by HM Customs Officers. It was, he recalls in his autobiography *The Eye of the Wind*, very damp and basic when he took it over, but during the years that he lived there he added a flat-roofed studio overlooking the marshes, a larger bathroom and a bunkroom connected with the boathouse. He was there not only to paint birds but also to collect them and eventually house them in the wildfowl centres which he

Lighthouse at Guy's Head, once the studio of Sir Peter Scott

was then trying to establish in other parts of the country, including the one at nearby Peakirk. Many of the geese liked the pens he had provided for them at Guy's Head and returned of their own free will, knowing they would always be well fed.

It was at the lighthouse that he was able to develop his own style of capturing on canvas the movements of birds, day after day:

> I was also brimming over with ideas. I could not wait until one picture was finished before starting the next ... I painted in bouts of intense energy, working all day and long into the night, with two Aladdin mantle lamps, one at either side of the canvas.

Now the artist himself is commemorated, not only by the plaque on the lighthouse but also by the Wash Coastal Path which is called The Peter Scott Walk, ten miles of breathtaking wildness from Guy's Head to West Lynn ferry. For a little over two hours, or more if you dawdle, one can breathe in the smell of salt and samphire and listen to the ever-changing chorus of bird-cries echoing over the estuary. It is a healing process not to be missed. The lungs, eyes, ears and soul are wonderfully restored.

Having completed our walk we returned to the car to collect our picnic-basket, then chose a suitable place on the river bank to enjoy a glass of wine and the food we had brought for the occasion. It was one more day to celebrate, one more day in the Fens to add to the already well-stocked treasury. And there was still the slow drive home to come, with the light growing ever more golden.

We were not to be disappointed. Because of the hot, dry summer there were already the first tell-tale dust clouds on the horizon, announcing that the mighty combines were commencing harvest. It is always a wonderful sight. All those months of growing, ripening, planning and (who knows?) praying, culminating in this most ancient of rituals known to man.

But how it has changed! Personally I am never sorry to see machines take the place of hard physical labour yet I have to accept that even the most practical of persons would agree that a lot of the romance has gone out of harvest and, with it, a great deal of social history and tradition. But, I ask myself, was it ever romantic? My grandfather would not have thought so. He came home too often from a day of reaping or stooking, his arms lacerated by the sharp corn stubble, to see it as anything other than painful, gruelling work. Nostalgia has made it what it is. Memories recall the friendly customs, the whole village's involvement and sense of well-being that a good harvest brought, if only for a short while. Bills and rents could now be paid. New tools, new clothes could be bought for the year to come. The silent stooks reflecting the evening sun spoke of fulfilment and the freedom to go gleaning when all but one of the stooks had been carted away. My mother often spoke of gleaning as 'the crumbs from a rich man's table' and I can remember going with her into the fields until it grew too dark to see. It was inevitable that such scenes of harvest should inspire artists, diarists and poets, but few of them would have sweated in the fields to achieve that appealing sight on canvas or on the page.

Although harvest scenes as such are with us no more I still get a thrill out of the first signs of each year's reaping, for that was what the combines were doing in their own calculated way. Those early dust clouds rising into the sky spoke of one thing. We had used the earth and the time well. As the day ended there was something not unlike the smell of incense in the air. The transparent light softened and the edges of the sky began to look slightly scorched. Embers of a day well spent, for all of us.

By the time we arrived home it felt as if we had travelled through half our century, that, for a moment, we had been where the minute-hand of time's clock paused, and then moved on.

As if to confirm my impression of an exceptionally abundant harvest that year, a report appeared in the national press a few days later, saying that farmers were working flat out from dawn to dusk, gathering one of the best wheat harvests in Britain for decades. Not only in the Fens but also in Suffolk, Norfolk, Yorkshire and other parts of the country, nature had been magnanimous. It was already estimated that the total grain yield would be one million tons higher than the twenty million tons of the year before, and that its value would be £2.4 billion, if not more. A world shortage of cereals was pushing up prices and British farmers were expecting to receive £127 a ton for bread-making wheat and £115 a ton for grain which would go towards animal foods. What was just as interesting was the fact that this output could have been ever higher had the EU not placed restrictions on production, instructing that 12 per cent of all arable land be set aside until further consideration the following year.

Now, in the spring of 1996 as this book is being prepared for publication, it is possible to say that most of those predictions were accurate. In a year that was to break several records I can understand why I saw so many happy farmers. The summer had certainly been heaven for those who had grown cereals.

I have to confess that I reduced that estimated tonnage by at least two grammes for I had surreptitiously plucked two ears of wheat to rub in my hands, blowing away the chaff as my grandfather had shown me, then chewing the warm, nutty grain, thereby bridging again a thousand years between modern technology and man's primitive attempts to feed himself and his family. That year, it seemed, we were about to feed the world.

2   Where Grisly Deeds
Were Dreamt of

There are still places in the Fens that one passes by on the way to somewhere else, quiet villages at the dead-ends of roads, small communities that go on with their own daily and seemingly uneventful lives, with hardly any recognition from the busy world. After all these years I find it hard to believe that there are still fenland villages I have not been to, even though it would not have taken me more than a mile or two off my chosen route to do so.

Such a place is the village of Christchurch, near Upwell. I have been many times to Christchurch in Dorset and my wife has been to Christchurch in New Zealand on as many occasions, but until recently we had never got as far as the one in Cambridgeshire. We had passed the end of its road scores of times on our way to Welney but had never been tempted to make a diversion to see what was at the other end.

The approach is not only a familiar one but also among my favourite drives. The road from Chatteris to Upwell along the lengthy Sixteen Foot Drain is an impressive stretch of fenland – spacious fields, bright water, immense skies and scattered farmsteads. Then, turning off towards Welney, the road dips and narrows with an air of secrecy into a territory that is unmistakable fen. I remember taking this route a couple of winters ago with two friends, Sue and Trevor Hold, who wanted me to introduce them to the Fens and the Wildfowl Centre at Welney. Occasionally they drew my attention to the road-signs we passed – ROAD CLOSED! FLOODS! I tried to reassure them by saying that we were sometimes a bit dilatory in taking down our signs and that they were probably left from last year. But, by the time we reached the village of Welney, I realized the error of my ways. The floods were well and truly out and we could not get beyond the village hall. 'Never mind' I said, 'we'll park the car here and walk across.' Sue and Trevor raised their eyebrows with an expression of concern that suggested they did not have complete faith in my divine talents. I stood at the water's edge and pondered. The floods were almost a mile wide and three feet deep. There was no way we could get over.

We were about to turn back when a lorry appeared from a nearby farm and headed towards the bridge. I flagged it down and asked the driver if he could ferry us across to the other side. 'Well, if you're prepared to risk it, I am. At least you'll be able to give me a push if we get stuck.' We climbed up over the muddy wheel and into the cab, then inched our way into the water which was soon level with the cab door. There was a wooden shelf above the dashboard on which lay an assortment of vegetables, like a mini harvest festival. I asked the driver if he would like us to sing 'All is safely gathered in'. He smiled and said, 'It's surprising what you see lying by the side of the road these days.'

We eventually reached the dry side of the bridge and could see that the path down to the Wildfowl Centre was clear. As we clambered down from the cab we thanked our ferryman for saving the day. 'That's all right. Mind you, I don't know how you're goona git back. This is my last trip today. Master's calling us all in. Says the floods are gooin' to git worse.'

As he drove off towards Ely I looked at my friends and saw what I sensed was a flicker of panic. I looked back over the bridge and realized that my car was now in the village cut off by a growing depth of water. However, there was nothing we could do about it and so we cheerfully set off, singing and joking as we walked the mile and a bit to the Wildfowl Centre. There we had some hot soup and homemade bread before going over to the hides to watch the birds. It was a wonderful sight because, despite the floods, the day was fine and there was a golden light over the water. There were also thousands of birds and Sue and Trevor had great fun seeing how many species they could identify.

Two hours later, and with the light fading quickly, we

decided that we had better come to terms with the problem of getting back to the car. 'You should start praying that there is just one lorry that hasn't been called in,' said Trevor, 'otherwise we shall have to swim across.' That would have presented me with an even greater problem, but I didn't let on.

We must have waited nearly half an hour before a lorry appeared out of the blue and turned on to the bridge. Again, I asked the driver if he would kindly ferry us over to the village, which he did. 'I'm having quite an interesting day,' he told us. 'I've just got back from delivering a load of black fen soil to Buckingham Palace.' There was a moment's silence in which he noticed our looks of disbelief, so he produced from his pocket a delivery note signed by the head gardener. 'And now I've got you,' he said, as if we were an anti-climax.

With considerable relief I saw my car still parked where I had left it in the morning and asked our driver to set us down near the village hall. I am certain he considered our exploits to have been rather crazy for our age and as we said goodbye he looked at me with some concern. 'Now you do know which way you're going, don't you?' I assured him that we would keep to dry land all the way home. I suppose there are gentler ways of introducing people to the Fens but, as we drove towards Manea under a red marbled sky, I convinced myself that my guests were not disappointed to have shared in the day's drama.

But already this unintentional digression looks as if I am still destined never to get to Christchurch. To do so I must return to that record-breaking summer day and this time take the appropriate road into the village which I now wanted to visit for a special reason.

My first impression was that we were not the only ones who had passed Christchurch by for it had the atmosphere of a place untouched by the events of the last fifty years. Let me assure its inhabitants that this is said as a compliment and not a criticism. No doubt they would say that there have been too many changes, but for me it was like stepping back into the leisurely era of a childhood summer. The morning was peaceful and unhurried. A man was clipping his garden hedge. A lady was cutting flowers. The cottage gardens were a mixture of plants and vegetables. Doors and windows were open, and I was sure that the corner shop was going to smell of sherbet and homemade lemonade.

My reason for wanting to make this belated visit was to bring together the other place in the Fens' associations with the writer Dorothy L. Sayers, for it was here that her father was rector from 1917–28 and where she wrote some of her early detective stories. What is not so well known is that her first two publications were slim volumes of poetry.

Her connections with the Fens began at Bluntisham, near Earith, where her father was the rector from 1897–1917. Dorothy was born in Oxford in 1893 so was only four years old when her family moved to the large, elegant house in Cambridgeshire, a notable change from the society they had been used to. It was in this village of less than 900 people that she had her first contact with the stubborn fenland character as well as the wild landscape around her. Those local people still had dramatic stories to tell of burst river-banks, floods and severe winters, and the writer was to draw on all these events in her novels, especially in *The Nine Tailors* (1934). She may not have loved the Fens as some people do, but she was fascinated by them and took some trouble to inform herself as much about the history of drainage as she did about bell-ringing.

By the time she came to write that novel she had also learnt just how parochial people in the Fens could be, even in times of disaster, refusing to allow flood-water from one parish to flow through the next because it would increase the risk of flooding there. As she was to get Lord Peter Wimsey to remark, 'What with seven hundred years of greed and graft and laziness, and perpetual quarrelling between one parish and the next ... the thing's a mess.' Harsh words for an outsider, maybe, but Miss Sayers was never afraid to speak her mind. She was to have as many mixed feelings about Christchurch as she'd had about Bluntisham but, being more mature now, she was able to make good use of the material she found there. In one of her letters she said that not only was it the 'last place God made' but when he'd finished he found 'He'd forgotten the staircase.' This comment, however, did not stop her friends from coming to see her.

The rectory was considerably smaller than the one at Bluntisham and the brick church lacked the grandeur of

The Rectory at Christchurch, near Welney

those buildings she had been used to at Oxford during her years at the university. Although one of her biographers, Janet Hitchman, described the church as 'a mean little red building with an even meaner red brick rectory' I have to say that I found both attractive. On that Monday morning the church had an air of serenity and plainness about it that appealed to me. On the wall behind the font is a plaque which reads:

In Grateful Memory of the Service of
HENRY SAYERS, PRIEST,
From 1917–1928, Rector of this Parish,
And of Helen Mary, his Wife.
This tablet
Is placed by the parishioners.

My visit was enhanced by meeting a charming young

couple who were to be married there the following
Saturday. Their friendliness typified the nature of the
village and I was greeted with similar courtesy when I
went to the rectory, which is now a Christian conference
and retreat centre. Again, the unhurried air of tranquillity
filled the place and the flowered gardens gave no hint of
meanness. In fact it was hard to imagine how the young
novelist could have dreamt up such grisly deeds in her
secluded room. The first story she wrote there was *Whose
Body?* which starts with the discovery of a middle-aged
corpse in a bath. The first sentence alone was enough to
shock her readers of the day: ' "Oh damn!" said Lord
Peter Wimsey at Piccadilly Circus ...' But Dorothy was
used to shocking people. If she had ambivalent feelings
about Christchurch, its population was equally puzzled by
her as she rode about the countryside dressed like a
gypsy, smoking in public. She bought her cigarettes at the
corner shop and frequented the local pub, the Dun Cow.
Often she was seen walking along the dykeside or sitting
on a river-bank writing and smoking for hours. She
shocked the villagers even more by arriving at the rectory
one day on a motor-bike when she was already six months
pregnant. She kept this news, and the name of her lover, a
secret until after the birth. It was some time before she
confessed that the father was Bill White, the man who had
first aroused her interest in motor-bikes.

With Britain still trying to recover from the aftermath of
the First World War there were to be many social changes
during the next decade. Dorothy was still not sure what
she wanted to do with her life. She had tried teaching,
both in Hull and in France, which must have been almost
the extremes of the educational spectrum. She had
worked in publishing and had been surprisingly
successful in a man's world as a copywriter for an
advertising agency. Her most popular caption was the
simple phrase 'Guinness is Good for You', but she also
extolled the virtues of Fynnon's Salt, shoe-polish and
Laxamalt. Above all, though, she wanted to be a writer
and, slowly, book by book, established herself as one of
the leading crime-writers of her day, surpassed only by
Agatha Christie.

When she came to draw on the Fens as a setting for her
detective stories she was determined to be as accurate and

as knowledgeable about them as she could. She had clearly read Charles Kingsley on the subject and gets in a gentle dig at him when she has Lord Peter Wimsey say in *The Nine Tailors*, 'I bet that when Kingsley welcomed the wild north-easter he was sitting indoors by a good fire, eating muffins.' Her own preference was for winter and it was a season she made excellent use of in her writing. The closing pages of that novel contain some splendid descriptions of the fears and dramas of an expected flood in the village. Knowing how helpless they will be when the banks break the villagers hurriedly gather together what essential belongings they can carry and seek refuge in the church tower, whose solid walls will give them protection. It is a scene that has been played out in reality on many occasions.

I went back to the church for a second impression and still liked it. The sanctuary, shaped like the stern of a ship, and the intricate timbered roof, reverberated for a moment with the eloquent sermons of the gentle, scholarly Reverend Henry Sayers, who probably understood his eccentric, free-thinking daughter more than she realized.

My wife and I then walked round the village to find the little wooden post-office from where I wished to dispatch a package that would not go through the letter-box just outside. The post-mistress and a customer were discussing diets and, in particular, how difficult it was to eat and lose weight at the same time – a common dilemma. Waiting, even in a queue of one, is not my favourite pastime but in Christchurch, what did it matter how long it took? I was enjoying the seriousness of the conversation as well as its humour.

'I shall probably have to wait until I take my place in the churchyard before I start to lose weight!' said the customer.

'You're right!' said the post-mistress. 'So what's the point of starving yourself to death until you get there!'

They then looked at me and decided that I should not be party to this intimate conversation. I quickly explained that I only wanted to hand in my package, already stamped, which I could not get through the letter-box. The customer took it from me and passed it to the post-mistress, saying, 'She'll see that gets off before Christmas.'

With that reassurance I left and went back to the car. From Christchurch we drove through the long and attractive village of Upwell, then took the back road down to Lakesend and Welney. In the sultry leafy summer Upwell had a very strong Dutch feel about it, with a canal running through the centre of the village and some pleasant houses either side. The parish church of St Peter's, together with St Wendreda's in March and Terrington St Clements near King's Lynn, gave Dorothy L. Sayers all the details she wanted for her imaginary Fenchurch St Paul in *The Nine Tailors* – a church which she nevertheless had specially designed for her by the architect W.J. Redhead.

From Welney we made our leisurely way back towards Chatteris. The expansive plains were as dry and as dusty as the prairies. It was impossible to find any shade for our picnic. Again the predominance of the crops was wheat and I was beginning to long for a patch of green to relieve the monotony. When it did come it was a field of onions which had just been pulled and laid out in rows to dry beneath the sun, their pale bulbous shapes already turning brown. Although I have no personal experience of the place I had the idea that this was probably what a beach looked like at Benidorm. There were to be other fields of onions on later trips but they now all looked the same – rows of half-naked sun-worshippers, peeling. This part of the Isle of Ely is not typical Fen country. It has more contours and more trees. From Little Downham and Wardy Hill one gets some elevated views across the rest of the Fens which are most attractive. It may have been the winter landscape that inspired Dorothy L. Sayers more than summer but I was grateful that, because of her, I had finally been to Christchurch and was then witnessing the second day of a great harvest.

As those weeks passed the summer began to look as if we were never to reach another winter. Grazing land became parched and cracked. Reservoirs dried up. Hose-pipes were banned and gardens wilted. Soon the trees appeared limp and dehydrated. Their leaves would surely not amaze us that year with a feast of colour. We were beginning to think that there would be no autumn either. With our national obsession about the weather we all longed for rain, for a reminder of the Fens as Dorothy

L. Sayers had described them, where 'road and dyke marched on side by side into an eternity of winter'. But an eternity is a long time, and who would want any season to last forever? There were, as we were to find out, changes on the way.

3 Out of the Blue

When I published my first book on the Fens more than twenty-five years ago all kinds of doors began to open for me. Nothing over spectacular but attractive enough to tempt me away from my desk once or twice a week. I was soon being invited to give talks, open garden fetes, visit schools and read many diaries or memoirs kept by other people in the hope that one day they too would get their books published. Sometimes there were real finds and I was grateful for the privilege of sharing in their experiences. As subsequent books have shown I also gained some very good friends. But I think my initiation into being a guest speaker at the Women's Institute meetings must remain one of my favourite memories of those innocent years.

That particular branch of the movement was deep in the Fens and it was a cold November night. I arrived, as instructed (or so I thought), at half-past seven. As I entered the hall an important-looking lady asked who I was and then informed me that they would not be ready for me until ten-past eight because the business matters had to be discussed first. I said that was quite all right and would settle down with a book in the corner of the room until they were ready. I was then told that the business matters were discussed in private and it would be better if I came back later. But where do you go in a remote fenland village on a damp November night, until later?

I stepped out of the hall into the deserted street and looked for the nearest pub. When I found it there was only one other customer in the bar. I said good evening but had no reply. I ordered my drink and sat down at a nearby table. 'Not many in tonight,' I said. He shook his head in morose agreement but spoke not a word. 'Do you come here often?'

Again he shook his head but this time managed to grunt
'no'.

I tried again. 'Then why are you here tonight?'

He suddenly came to life. 'I brought the missus up to a
meeting. They've got some silly bugger coming to talk to
them about the Fens.' I was the one who was now
speechless. Later, when I was finally allowed into the
village hall, I could not resist telling the ladies what had
happened and the one who had turned me out went a
deep crimson. It was her husband in the pub.

I am able to tell this story now (and often do) because
over the years I have built up a very friendly relationship
with the WI and, by a calculated guess, would say that I
have been to more than seventy of their branches in East
Anglia. Often I gain more than I give for they all have their
characters, women who have worked in the Fens for years
and know all the local history there is to know. It all
proved to be both fun and informative and, again, I was
frequently invited into some of their homes to talk at
greater length.

The more people I met the more convinced I was that
true fen-dwellers were a nation apart – stubborn,
independent and quietly proud. One could no longer call
them 'the last Englishmen' for that distinction had gone
out with Hereward the Wake. Since the eleventh century
more than the Normans have infiltrated into this last
stronghold of old England. The Dutch, French, Scottish
and Italians have all introduced their own characteristics
and, eventually, cross-breeding to change the population.
It is difficult now to say who we are. But, even if it is no
longer possible to find a pure strain, I still feel that I am
getting very close to some of the original fenmen that I
have read about in earlier histories, men and women who
were even more fiercely independent, suspicious, hard-
working, rough and ready, and no respecters of other
people, whatever their status. They seldom made
concessions, and still don't. One has to establish a
relationship with them on their own terms. But once that
has been achieved they are a warm, generous and loyal
people. I grew to admire them enormously and tried to
resurrect some of those old qualities in myself. I had a
feeling they were there but had been submerged under
the many other influences I had received since childhood.

Uneventful though it was, my life had not been anywhere near as insular as those of the people I was now beginning to meet. Some seldom left their villages more than once a year. Some were farming the land that had been farmed by their forefathers for many generations. It was not unusual to meet people in their eighties who had never moved more than two hundred yards from where they were born. Many of them would still not be told what to do and one, to this day, still refuses to wear a seat-belt, even though he has been fined half a dozen times. When the cold, blue eye of a fenman looks defiant he does not have to use the word 'no'.

This could be seen as stupidity rather than stubbornness but it is another example of their stern refusal to be pushed around. They will tell you that they have quite enough to put up with from nature without any bureaucratic interference. Because they also like to protect themselves against the elements as much as possible, they usually grow tall hedges or rows of closely planted trees round their houses to serve as a shield, especially against the winds that rage across their open lands like an invisible high tide. Even the most solid houses can seem to shudder and quake at such buffetings. More than once I have been hustled in from a gale for a welcoming cup of tea on a winter's afternoon. The trees which create these individual little oases can also soften the starkness of the houses and, on calm summer evenings, will attract the golden light of the setting sun until they look mellow if not beautiful. On such occasions one arrives at a scene romantic enough for a legend. Nowhere in this country can the sun's rays get lower and still flood the land with their light. Ely Cathedral, for instance, can look celestial from miles away when lit by the last beams of a late June evening.

I have frequently made the point that each book I write soon becomes a passport to someone else's life and it is one of the rewards of the job. Somewhere, from out of the blue, a person writes to me and I find a new story waiting to be told. And what impresses me most about these letters is the ability of each writer to recall so vividly the events and people of fifty years ago, even though they may not have been back to renew their acquaintance, at least not physically. Many, I am sure, have returned in spirit and still retain an affection for the place of their childhood and early years. How else could they write, as Mr Albert Bird from Southport did a few months ago? After some kind comments about my book *Fen Boy First* he went on to say:

A number of your experiences in the town of Whittlesey were very similar to mine. We went to the same schools, walked the same streets, and I knew some of the people you mention ... I was born at King's Dyke in 1918, in the little black wooden railway house at the railway-crossing. My father had been a signalman there since 1895. My eldest brother, Percy, who was in the First World War, was a burner at Itter's brickyard. My next brother, Arthur, after working as a gate boy at Whittlesea Station, was later employed driving a small diesel engine at the Central Brick Company ... I left that awful place – the Whittlesey C of E Senior Boys' School, in 1932 when I was fourteen. My first job was working for Ted Smith as a milk boy, going round the town with a three-gallon milk bucket with a lid. When it was full it was extremely heavy and for a week of nearly seventy hours I was paid eleven shillings. When Mr Smith heard that I had applied for a job at the Co-op he gave me the sack. So I became a grocer's apprentice and it seemed like heaven after milking five cows, cleaning out the cow-sheds, and lugging a heavy milk pail round the town. The most wonderful thing of all was that I got a half-day off and eventually played football for Whittlesey Thursday Athletic Club, with a very good player called Curly Rippon. As I say, you mention quite a number of people I still remember – Flowery George, who always wore a button-hole; Theo Bingham, the baker and confectioner. My sister worked for him, and his nephew – Albert Bingham, was best-man at my wedding. I also remember Rowdy Dick, a drover, who, if we teased him on our way to school, would threaten us with his stick. Then there was Fireman Fiddy, the harness maker in Station Road. He was captain of the local fire brigade. He was reported to have said on one occasion, 'Quick. Run after the milkman. I've lent him our horse and there's a fire out at Eldernell.' [This was about three miles from the town.]

Yes we had our characters all right. Did you by any chance know a bus-driver by the name of Chicken Hemmingway? He worked for the then Eastern Counties Bus Company and had such an infectious laugh that it could be heard all over the Market Place. The incident I remember most clearly was one morning when Chicken, on his usual 8.40 run to Peterborough, stopped at the house of Mr Dickie Winters, the music teacher, in Broad Street. Every Wednesday and Friday Dickie used to go to Stanground for the day to teach some of his pupils and to play for a service in the church. Often he was late but it made no difference. Chicken Hemmingway would always wait for him. Sometimes Mrs Winters would come to the door with a cup of tea in her hand and her husband would hastily drink it before getting on to the bus. On this particular morning he was later than usual and when he did appear, Chicken exploded into one of his most infectious laughs. All the passengers looked out to see what the matter was, and there was Dickie Winters, trilby hat on, overcoat buttoned up, a music-case in his hand, and his long-johns showing below his coat. He had come out without his trousers.

Although twelve years younger than Albert Bird I can vouch for these characters and the stories that went with them. Mr Winters was a delightful little man, rather Pickwickian in appearance with a beaming smile and steel-rimmed spectacles. He was a harmless eccentric and there are numerous anecdotes about him. I once saw him standing under a tree with his umbrella up during a light shower. When I asked him why he was sheltering there he looked surprised and said he did not want to get his brolly wet. He also had a habit of borrowing heavy volumes from the public library, not to read, but to stack on the bass end of his piano to stop the lower notes vibrating. His benign, shining face was as essential to the town as any of its landmarks. He is one of our immortals.

Albert Bird's letter continued with memories of the many activities that kept people amused in those days – the Buffaloes' Dance, the Cricket Club Dance and the Police Concerts, with Norman Long the comedian topping the bill. He was still going strong when I went to my first National Farmers' Union dinner.

Like most exiled fenmen, Albert also had his stories about the favourite winter pastime, skating:

I remember the rivers freezing over and skating from King's Dyke to Black Bridge and back. Skating matches were held on Whittlesey Wash and the jeweller, 'Clockie' Norris, gave 5/- watches as prizes to the young skaters ...

So much comes back to me now and I can still visualize walking to school at King's Dyke when I was five. There Miss Rose taught us and we learned to read and write with a slate and slate-pencil. I don't remember seeing any books, and we were taught to count, to add up and subtract, by the use of shells. At the age of seven I left the Infants' School and had to walk all the way into Whittlesey to attend the Junior School in Broad Street ...

And another thing I remember was a series of epidemics and the schools had to be closed. I think it was about 1928 or '29. We hardly went to school that summer. Scarlet Fever, Small Pox, Diphtheria. Many of the pupils at Station Road School were vaccinated and wore red arm-bands to avoid having their arms knocked ...

When I look back at my time at that school I feel angry. What an awful school it was. Unhygienic, cold in winter, and us boys from King's Dyke were locked out at dinner time so that we had nowhere to eat our packed dinners. The school didn't even have a water tap for drinking, and then, like you, that awful trauma of being sent to March for the 'eleven-plus' exam for which we received no preparation at all. I shall never forget the tenseness of the journey by train – the first train journey I had ever taken without my parents – and the dreadful atmosphere of the exam room in a strange building ...

But, despite his very meagre formal education, Albert Bird went on to better himself and to become an excellent teacher, gaining a degree and rising to deputy head of the English department of a large high school, where he was also the librarian.

This is but one example of the interesting letters I receive and it would appear that Whittlesey, and the Fens in general, stay in people's blood for years after they have left. Before moving on to other subjects I must mention one more letter because it came from a lady who now lives in Wiltshire but who taught me when I was six and a pupil at the Broad Street Infants' School mentioned by Mr Bird.

Mrs Evelyn Merritt was then a very young Miss Evelyn Hart, daughter of a well-known local farming family. I know she was young because she also sent me a photograph of the school staff taken in 1936 and, apart from the headteacher, Miss Cole – who looked suitably fierce – the rest could easily pass for senior schoolgirls. I suppose they all appeared old to us then but Evelyn could have been no more than twenty-one or -two. But she remembered me and those early days of her career before she married and moved down to the West Country:

> When my husband died in 1990 I went back to Whittlesey, back to my roots, where I absorbed so much strength and will to carry on from Blackbush. Do you remember in *Gone With the Wind* when Rhett leaves Scarlett, she says 'I'll go back to Tara tomorrow'? I thought of that quite often. It was amazing that after my visit to the site of the old house in Reach Drove I seemed to see things in better perspective. Like you I heard voices of the past, the noises of the cattle, horses etc., the wind blowing through the farm buildings. But now there is nothing. Every thing has gone – house, buildings, livestock, just nothing but the land ...

Who would have thought that my kind Infants' School teacher, Miss Hart, would turn up again sixty years later as one of my readers, more than a little surprised, perhaps, that I had progressed beyond that ordinary small boy who spent most of his time staring out of the classroom window and never did manage to get his shells to add up to the right total. What is it that finally pulls all these fragile strands to their centre? Nothing but the land? Those who, like Evelyn, are drawn back to their roots know there is something more. We belong to a time as well as a place, and paths that were once crossed have a habit of re-crossing many years later.

Shortly after receiving that letter I went out to Blackbush, to where I had also spent some very happy hours as a child and was reminded that if my Fen country heaven was anywhere, it was there where I first knew the joy, freedom and contentment of being able to roam under those vast skies, picking wild flowers, listening to larks and watching the silver fish flash like shooting stars in the shallow stream.

It was along that narrow bumpy road which appeared to lead to nowhere that I can remember my mother taking me when I was a small child to collect bulrushes. (We made the common mistake of giving them this name rather than the correct one of reed-mace but, as a boy, I knew them only as bulrushes and have called them so ever since.) Would they still be there, I wondered, sixty

Reed-mace – their long suede heads, ancient and brown

years later, erect as busbied grenadiers awaiting orders to
get into line? I recalled that they were always tantalizingly
out of reach and that my mother had to go down into the
deep dyke to cut them. It was all so long ago that I would
probably find even the dykes had gone. Although the road
was not far from where I live I had not been on it for more
than twenty years. But I had not travelled more than a
mile before I saw them, just as they'd always been. It was
as if I had taken a journey back to when I was six. Not only
were the dykes still as deep but there was a whole
regiment of bulrushes. In one dyke alone, no more than a
hundred yards long between one field-gate and another, I
counted 324. Mysterious, ancient and Cadbury-brown,
they epitomized an England that had hardly changed in a
thousand years. The sun lit up their long suede heads to
re-establish their right name of reed-mace. It was the same
in the dyke on the opposite side of the road. In the fields
beyond were great rolls of straw left from the harvest and I
was reminded again of those summer evenings an age ago
when my mother had taken me gleaning, in days when
the harvest was gathered in by hand. History? Legends?
Nostalgia? Regret? Relief? What else?

Eventually a middle-aged woman came along pushing
an old man in a wheel-chair. I could not see where they
had come from, or to where they might be going. Houses
were distant and sparse and there was no bend in the
road. They stopped to talk and I explained why I was
there, commenting on how little it had changed.

'Oh, yes, it 'as,' said the woman with considerable
authority. 'There's bin a lot of changes out 'ere in my time
– and 'is.' She nodded to the man in the wheel-chair, 'ain't
that right, dad?'

He gave a barely discernible nod of agreement and his
daughter said, 'He used to be a horse-keeper on Mr Rose's
farm. One of the best in the Fens.' I looked at him again
and suddenly he seemed to contain more than a hundred
years of fenland history.

So what sort of changes had taken place then within his
lifetime?

'Hedges,' said the woman. 'Years ago when we worked
on the land the fields had hedges. Now you can travel
twenty miles without seeing a hedge. They took 'em all
out to get more land and look what you got.' I looked

across the vast open landscape and could not remember any hedges. Had I uprooted them from my memory?

I then asked what other changes there had been, and she replied 'Horses! These fens used to be full of horses and landworkers. My father had some beauties – didn't you?' The old chap nodded. 'If it rained,' the woman explained, 'I could shelter between the horse's two front legs and I'd never git wet, it were that broad across the chest.'

Looking over the fields towards the distant brickyard chimneys I said that there were certainly not as many chimneys as there used to be. 'Well, you know why, don't you?' she said. 'Most of 'em was blowed up about ten years ago. It's all modernized now, like everything else. And nobody wants the bricks they do make these days.'

We then spoke briefly about the glorious day and the unusually hot weather for September. 'It were allus like this years ago,' she said. Maybe, I thought. We only remember what we do not wish to forget. I saw that she was looking at the camera in my hand. 'You won't take much with that out 'ere.' She was right, in a way. The Fens are the most difficult landscape to photograph. One can't really film space, or, for that matter, feelings.

I watched the couple as they resumed their journey, slowly receding like diminishing dots on the horizon. Yes, there had been a lot of changes, but the spirit of the place was undoubtedly still there, still vibrating in the soil and in the air. Echoes that had meaning. I knew exactly what Evelyn Merritt had felt like when she went back to her roots, to the farm in Reach Drove, Blackbush.

'Why,' I was to ask her later, 'was it called Reach Drove? Was it named after a person, or place?'

'I think it was probably an old English word,' she explained, 'meaning quagmire, or it could have simply meant it was once a bend in the river which ran close by. Certainly part of my father's farm was on the course of an early dyke which had been filled in and it was always wetter on that stretch of land than anywhere else. When he grew rye in that field it would always be nine inches taller than the rest of the crop.'

The unseen, unwritten history is still what fascinates and I often feel that the land is like a great detective story waiting to be solved. But, even knowing the little I do, I was aware that I had enjoyed a wonderful experience walking along that road about which I had been saying, 'I'll go back tomorrow.'

Now I had been and knew for certain I would return again soon, especially as the early days of autumn were promising days as golden as those of that perfect summer. It was as if all the best moments of my life in the Fens were coming together in one year.

4   Recognizing the Certainties

The landscape of the Fens, with its brooding mystery and grandeur has been the breeding-ground for many legends, reputations and distinguished people. I have already mentioned two in earlier chapters but there are others, and I am constantly surprised by the number of men and women who have made a lasting contribution to the story of the Fen country.

I was reminded again of this a few days ago as I drove along a country road that had just been re-surfaced. It may have looked a new road for a little while but no amount of tarmacadam could hide for ever an inch of our history. No white lines could succeed in obliterating the footprints of all those characters whose steps have passed over this land.

I was on my way to visit a primary school in Wimblington, a small fenland village near March and one that, like Christchurch, I had left behind on my way to somewhere else. But now I had been invited to work with the local schoolchildren, to encourage them to write about where they lived and what they thought of the surrounding landscape. Some of them were new to the area so I wondered how they felt about growing up in the Fens?

As there was very little traffic on the road I was able to take my time, stopping occasionally to re-acquaint myself with a familiar but ever-changing scene. It was as if each field was trying to outdo its neighbour, as if the earth was determined this year to prove to the world what it could do. As a farmer had said to me a few days before, 'You've got to admit, it does your heart good to see the land responding like that ...' Whilst he was probably suggest-

ing that he should take most of the credit I felt this was
praise indeed.

I had earlier passed a man with a horse and cart but, in
my dallying, he had caught up with me. We acknowledged each other's presence and I let him get well ahead
of me before continuing my journey, envying the slow
speed at which he would travel for the rest of the day.

Driving through the Fens that morning it occurred to me
that every village and town has a school or hall named
after some worthy whose legacy to the community had
been recognized in a practical way to help the future
remember them. The more I thought about it the more
aware I was of how difficult a task it would be to compile a
list of even the schools in the area named after such
famous local persons. The sky itself could hardly contain
such a roll-call of honour. Some names were naturally
familiar beyond our boundaries – Hereward the Wake,
Oliver Cromwell, Octavia Hill, John Clare and Edith
Cavell. Some of those individuals not only have schools
and village halls named after them, but car-parks! But
what of those lesser-known mortals whose achievements
might rest only in the places they enriched with their
talents or benevolence? For instance, the school in
Wimblington to which I was travelling was named after a
Mr Thomas Eaton. And who was he, I wondered?
Fortunately the headmaster, Mr Ross Davies, was more
than willing to answer that question and, furthermore, to
provide me with photocopies of several old documents
that were to add a bonus to my day with the children.

Thomas Eaton was a modest landowner and farmer
who was born in 1680 and died a bachelor in 1715 at the
age of thirty-five. It was not a long life in which to earn a
place in memory or to claim an inch of immortality but at
least he had done enough to have a school named after
him eventually. I say 'eventually' for a good reason. He
had made his will on 8 January 1714, leaving the majority
of his estate to Nicholas Richardson of Wimblington. The
property consisted of two houses with common rights and
several pieces of land which totalled no more than thirty
acres. Some items in the inventory of his goods and
personal effects made interesting reading:

	£ s d
In the Hall two Tables, Four Chaires a Dresser-Board & Pewter Case, a pair of Tongs & a Pair of Hooks	1 0 0
In the Chamber over the Hall, One Bedstead, a Flock Bed, 3 Blanketts, a Parll of Cheese, 2 Cheese Rackes, a parll of daglocks & a parll of Beanes	3 0 0
In the Garden 17 Skegges of Bees	5 19 0
More than Two Hundred Woolly Sheep	105 0 0

And so it went on, with no visible order to the value of things, but every possession, large or small, had its price. In the event of Nicholas Richardson dying without heirs, provision was made in the will for the erection of 'a free School in Wimblington' for the good of the community. As it happened, Mr Richardson did die without issue in 1734 and so the village looked forward to getting its first school. When, two years later, nothing had been done to carry out these intentions, a body of trustees was established to erect a building and to appoint a headmaster. But, one by one, the trustees themselves died and the legal rights to the estate became complicated if not confused. In 1802 a new trust was formed and the following resolutions were passed:

1 That one schoolroom and dwelling for the Master should be erected.
2 That the school should be for the use and benefit of children of the inhabitants of Wimblington, not exceeding 40 in total – boys and girls included.
3 That out of the rents of the estate the Trustees, apart from the maintenance of the School, should also provide books and stationery for the pupils and that should any surplus money become available it should be used for the improvement of the charity's estates or the purchase of annuities.
4 That the Trustees should elect a Schoolmaster capable of teaching children reading, writing and arithmetic. He was to be married and of good character and a member of the Church of England.
5 That the children should attend regularly Divine Service at Doddington Church.
6 That the children admitted to the School should not be

under the age of 6 years – boys to continue to the age of 14 years – girls not to remain after the age of 13 years.

Such plans, for their time, were quite progressive but affairs do not always move swiftly in the Fens and a start was not made on the proposed new building until 1815, a hundred years after Thomas Eaton's death. However, by the end of 1817 the school was erected for a cost of about £800 and, a year later, the first headmaster, Mr Benjamin Ward, was appointed at a salary of £60 per annum, to instruct the forty children in the manner desired.

He must have found it hard work trying to educate fenland children because after three years he resigned and the trustees closed the school. It re-opened in May 1824 with a new headmaster, Mr John Wright, for the same salary. From then on the school managed to survive and existing logbooks give some idea of what life was like in the village at that time.

23 July 1886: Several of the children are still in the habit of staying away on Fridays, the object in most case to earn two days' wages in the week.

6 December 1889: Measles Epidemic. 2 deaths. School closed for five weeks by order of the Medical Officer of Health.

20 April 1890: The first class is now rather small, some of the half-timers having started work.

30 April 1890: Owing to a serious outbreak of Scarlet Fever the school was closed today by order of the Medical Office of Health.

14 December 1891: The Infant Mistress – Miss Gibson, the Headmaster and his wife, and their daughter, all taken ill with 'drain fever' due to the bad drains.

16 February 1892: The attainments of the children here are very low – many parents keep their children away for any pretext. Some are in employment without any certificate whatever.

18 March 1892: Irregularity and illegal employment on the increase without rhyme or reason – Parents do as they please here.

Such stories are not unknown these days but a hundred years ago it was clearly no easy task for anyone trying to enlighten the community and similar logbook entries can be found in many parishes. I remember reading of one teacher who spent the morning 'teaching the children the use of soap' and of another who 'today went to the market to buy remnants of clothes for the children in my class who are ragged'.

In another school a girl was absent for several days 'because the clock fell on her head' and the reason given for one girl's absence was that her mother had just had a baby 'and the Attendance Officer knows all about it'. In one school the children stood in the playground in the snow, many of them in bare feet, waiting for the bishop to come and give them a Christmas blessing. The Black Death and cholera were mentioned frequently but, on a more cheerful occasion, the children were allowed to have the morning off to watch a circus parade through the town. It was a different world, but not so long ago.

What a changed picture it is today. The children I was to meet at Wimblington are taught in attractive, well-lit rooms under the wise guidance of their headmaster and his enthusiastic staff. The wide range of subjects, from Egyptology to Ecology, from World Religions to Computer Studies, impressed me. My task of getting the children to write about their landscape and the life around them could not have been easier. They responded with good humour to my unorthodox ways and by the end of the morning some excellent work had been produced, some of it most imaginative.

If it took a long time to put Thomas Eaton's wishes into practice it took even longer to get his name officially recognized by posterity, for the school was not named after him until 1960. I suppose some people have had to wait longer to be remembered and I am often reminded of Antony's words in *Julius Caesar* – 'The evil that men do lives after them,/The good is oft interred with their bones.' At least Wimblington has done its best now to make sure that the good intentions of one man are not forgotten.

Fortunately I was to be invited back again to the Thomas Eaton School and all my first impressions were confirmed. A press photographer was there to record the occasion and some more splendid work was done. When I asked the class if they had any more questions before I left one boy said, 'Do you ever get bored?'

I did not have to hesitate over the answer. 'Never,' I

Simple things take on a new significance

replied. 'Why, do you?'

He thought for a moment and then, tactfully trying to avoid saying that I had been guilty of boring him, said 'only sometimes'.

Driving home across that summer landscape I wondered how anyone could be bored. No two days are ever alike so even the familiar must appear different each time it is looked at by what John Clare called 'an unwearying eye'. Colours change, light varies, stillness creates a contrasting mood to that of movement and the simple things take on a new significance. Clouds are never the same shape or in the same place. Time flows. The circle is always turning.

Because I have always lived in the Fens I have been deeply affected by their space and light. People with only a cursory knowledge of the area will frequently comment on our wonderfully vast skies, and it is true that there is probably nowhere else in Britain where, on good days, one can experience such an incomparable dome of blue, or such large continents of cloud towering above the land, most of which is now below sea-level. But it is what those skies do to the land and the people that matters. They create the space and the light through which our thoughts can travel, even beyond the most distant horizons. I value that space which has been provided for me. I can walk along an unspoilt riverbank and find peace. I can stand overlooking a hundred acres of ripening wheat and absorb the stillness. I can still listen to skylarks or a passive wind rustling through the stalks of corn or barley and know that I am hearing the voice of eternity. I value the light too that enables me to stretch my vision beyond the concrete constructions of towns or cities. We do not have any mountains nearby to shut out the light, inspiring though mountains often are. For me they are still best where they belong, where nature put them. We have a different vista to appreciate. From horizon to horizon there appears to be little of interest or of beauty to the uninformed eye. But it is in that emptiness that I find the time and the silence in which to marvel at the many qualities that make life worth living. Other landscapes, of course, appeal to other minds. I only know that I am bound to value what has happened to me because of where it has happened. It's where the roots are and I take comfort in the words of Albert Camus – 'A man who can feel his links with one country, who knows that there is always a place where his heart will find its resting place, already owns many certainties in his life ... Everything at certain moments, yearns for the land of the soul,' from *Selected Essays & Notebooks* (Penguin 1979).

By a happy coincidence, on my second visit to Wimblington, I met again the man with the horse and cart. I had parked my car and was stretching my legs along the road between Angle Bridge and Benwick as he passed me. This time he spoke. 'Can't you make up your mind which way to go?' I assured him that I knew where I was going but was in no great hurry. 'That's all right then,' he said.

'How ever fast you go, go slowly is what I say.' And slowly he went on to wherever he was going. I decided to wait a few minutes before getting into the car.

5   Days of Discovery

Having salved my conscience by at last visiting the villages of Christchurch and Wimblington with such satisfying results, I felt it was worth trying the same kind of journey to another fenland community which had not previously lured me into its fold. Again I had been close when visiting neighbouring Soham and Prickwillow and, some years ago, must have moored just a rope's length away when we had a holiday on the River Lark. But the village of Isleham itself was still unknown to me and so I made up my mind to add it to my knowledge.

It is almost as far east as one can get in the Cambridgeshire Fens. The river helps to fix the county boundary and beyond that is Suffolk. It is as if the Fens themselves ran out of character there for the soil never looks as rich as the black fields to the north-west. Nevertheless, when our destination was eventually reached after a few digressions along the way, we were in for a delightful surprise. I must not, however, write about the end of our journey before saying something about the route there.

I get so used to driving into the Fens from the west, via Thorney or Crowland to the north, or Chatteris to the south, that it makes a change to approach them from the more elevated roads that go through Warboys, Pidley, Oldhurst, Bluntisham and Earith. From those villages one can see the Fens spread out, as John Clare said, 'like a map', a patchwork of colours that gives the appearance of having been patiently embroidered by hand, so tidy does the land look.

At Bluntisham we were to be reminded of our visit to Christchurch and the connections with Dorothy L. Sayers. At Earith there were the reminders too of the early attempts by Cornelius Vermuyden and the Gentlemen Adventurers to drain the Fens. The Old and the New Bedford Rivers – as those long, ambitious drains were to be called – were docile compared with what they can be like in a bad winter when floods threaten with as much menace as they did 300 years ago.

Continuing from Earith to Haddenham one can still be surprised by the height of some of the neighbouring villages such as Sutton-in-the-Isle for instance, which appears to be built on a hill. By Fen standards it is, for, like so many fenland communities, it was once an island. The local people even refer to these villages as the Fenland Alps and, for a person visiting the area for the first time, the terrain can be misleading. As a visitor from Wales once said to me 'I expected the Fens to be much flatter than this.'

'Don't worry,' I replied, 'they are.'

It was not my intention to visit Wicken Fen on this latest trip but, as the summer's day was so perfect and it was still only mid-morning, I decided it would make an ideal break in our journey. Although I had been to that National Trust property in the Fens many times before, my previous two visits had been on lingering, wet days. The droves that criss-crossed it were then very squelchy and the peat smelt sourly ancient. Now we were about to experience it during one of the hottest summers of the century and the change was to be dramatic. The dykes were dry. The reed-beds rustled like satin gowns in the warm wind and we could have been approaching a tropical jungle, so thick was the undergrowth. But it was still a fascinating place and the deeper we walked into the interior the more removed from the twentieth century we felt. There were occasional glimpses of water but it was the colour of flat Guinness.

One of the features of Wicken Fen is the attractive windmill which is, admittedly, now no more than a museum piece. It was removed from Adventurers' Fen and re-erected at Wicken to give us some idea of what it would have been like when hundreds of such mills were scattered over the whole of fenland. That was in the eighteenth century, when wind was the only power available to turn the sails which, in turn, worked the scooped wheels that raised the water from one level to

Preserved drainage windmill at Wicken Fen

another, from drain to river, and finally out to sea. But their days were numbered when the more efficient steam pumping stations took over in the late nineteenth century and they too gradually disappeared when electricity or diesel were introduced. Today the traveller through the Fens may catch sight of the occasional modern wind-turbines, which have a certain, futuristic grace but do not match the more leisurely beauty of the old sail mills.

Surprised that our diversion into the Fen had taken well over an hour, we quickly made our way back along the banks of Wicken Lode and then on to the busy main road again. But, before reaching Isleham, there was yet one more stop I wished to make in the bustling village of Soham. Some call it the largest village in the Fens, others say it is the smallest town. It has an excellent village college, a fine parish church, and an historic market. People wishing to dine out have the choice of Italian and Chinese meals as well as traditional fish and chips or the now ubiquitous pizza. And the local pubs serve bar meals too. It feels a very independent place.

I was no stranger to Soham and remembered especially my visit of the previous year when I gave the inaugural lecture in the new library which had recently been converted from the old Victorian school. The weather was hot on that occasion as well and when I arrived I was greeted by an audience of men in open-necked shirts and ladies in bright summer dresses. It was such a beautiful evening that I felt guilty at being the reason for their gathering in that ex-classroom when they could have all been outdoors playing bowls, or eating strawberries and cream in their gardens. At the same time, I was naturally grateful that so many of them were prepared to come and listen to me talking about the Fens. As there were some delightful Welsh and Scottish people there who had come to live in the area, I convinced myself that my mission was justified.

My reason for wanting to visit Soham again was to gather some information for a lady who had phoned me from Henley-on-Thames, asking if I had anything I could send her on the railway heroes of Soham, one of whom was an uncle or cousin. Fortunately the local bookshop had exactly what I was looking for, a recently published account by Anthony Day – *But For Such as These: The Heroes of the Railway Incident at Soham in 1944*. I bought a copy to send to the lady who had phoned but read it first.

It was a truly heroic and dramatic story that would have received more national coverage in the press had it not been overshadowed by the greater event of two days later – the D-Day invasion. During the Second World War large quantities of ammunition were conveyed by rail. When driver Benjamin Gimbert and fireman James Nightall reported for duty on 22 June 1944 they were aware that their trip was a particularly dangerous one, with fifty-one wagons, forty-four of which contained high explosives, mainly 500 lb bombs which were required by the RAF and American Air Force. The consignment had been on the move for three days since it was taken off ship on the Humber and now destined for White Colne in Essex. Gimbert and Nightall took over at March railway sidings that night and were approaching Soham station when the driver looked out of his cab and saw the first wagon on fire. He sounded his whistle to warn the guard and began the slow, careful task of stopping the train, which could not be braked sharply because of its cargo. The train was 390 yards long and the wagons heavily loaded. The consequences were only too obvious. There were only minutes in which to act.

Having brought his train to a standstill the driver told his fireman to uncouple the burning wagon from the rest so that they could tow it away into open country before it blew up. Ben Gimbert then slowed down at the station signal-box to tell the signalman, Frank Bridges, what was happening. But it was too late. Within seven minutes from the fire being spotted to that last moment of trying to avoid a disaster, more than five tons of explosives blew up, killing the signalman and the fireman outright, and hurling the driver two hundred yards down the track. The guard, Herbert Clarke, was also injured and the station demolished. Had such courageous action not been taken by those men the whole train-load of bombs could have gone off, with even more devastating results. Much of Soham would have been reduced to rubble and the cost of human lives counted in hundreds. The driver and the fireman were both to receive the George Cross. Sadly, for Jim Nightall the award was a posthumous one, but Ben Gimbert survived his injuries to collect his at an investiture at Buckingham Palace, though he is reported to have said at the time, 'Can't they put it through the letter-box?'

Satisfied with my find we were now able to continue our journey to Isleham down narrow roads with passing places, driving through clouds of straw dust from the adjacent combine-harvesters working along the edge of the fields. If I had a reason for going to Isleham for any other purpose than easing my conscience, it was to see if there were still any remains left of the Benedictine priory that was built there in 1090. Much of the building was, in fact, still intact even though the priory was suppressed in 1414 and was subsequently used as a barn and cattle-shed. That, and the nearby garage, seemed to sum up the difference that five centuries can make.

What was to be more of a surprise was the impressive parish church which was spacious, high, light and clean, with a magnificent hammer-beamed angel roof forty-seven feet above the floor. The ten large angels with their great wings bear the emblems of Christ's Passion. The lofty clerestory gave the impression of the nave walls always reaching up even higher for light. Originally there

One of the angels in the roof of Isleham Church

were sixty angels which must have made a more spectacular impact when the church was in its prime. Immediately inside the church was a large table made of Fen bog-oak and in the chancel were return stalls and a choir bench dated 1350, on which initials had been carved many years ago, presumably by bored choristers who had lost interest in the long sermon. There were also 15th-century brasses, some splendid ancestral tombs and a funeral sword that was originally buried with Sir Robert Peyton, in 1590. It was a wonderful discovery and a church I am now delighted to add to my list of fenland riches.

By now Isleham had the air of a Spanish village enjoying a siesta. It was hard to appreciate that within living memory it had nineteen pubs, eighteen market gardeners, twelve bird-snarers, its own brass band and a quoits club.

How our villages have changed in less than a hundred years! The great price paid by every community during the First World War must be one of the most important factors that led to such a rapid social upheaval in the early part of this century. In Isleham several families had three of its men killed during the 1914–18 War and further sacrifices were to be made by the next generation during 1939–45. We have to accept that life would not have stood still without those conflicts but the development of society would surely have been different.

So the villages change and sleep on to await another hundred years and we left Isleham to enjoy its siesta undisturbed. By which time the pangs of hunger were reminding us that we were still mortal and in need of something to eat. Finding that the nearby inn was not serving lunch that day we had the choice of driving up to Prickwillow or making tracks back to Stretham, where we knew we could get a meal at the Lazy Otter riverside inn, even at two o'clock. We sat outside to watch the boats. At the table next to us were two people from Christchurch, New Zealand. Naturally I urged them to visit Christ-church in Cambridgeshire but, for some reason, they had to get to Enfield and wouldn't have the time – 'Not that we really want to leave this spot,' they said.

Nor did we, but we at least had plenty of time to idle our way back over the Fens until the best part of the day was spent. And the longer one can stay out in the Fens the better because the light is often at its best towards evening. Its mellowness gives sharper definition to distant buildings. The fields seem to breathe more contentedly. It is a time when the rivers give back their light to the sky.

Although the day was over I had convinced myself that the days of discovery could never end even when everything appears so familiar. I felt like the farmer who said to me, 'It doesn't matter how many times I plough the same field, I always keep my eyes open, just in case one of these days the plough will turn up something glistening in the soil and I'll find it's Roman treasure.'

I still had quite a few fields to go but some kind of premonition told me to stay alert. There were things in the Fens I had not yet seen or heard about – events unplanned, people as yet unmet and buried treasure waiting to be found.

As some of the following chapters will show, my optimism was to be rewarded.

6   If Hilgay is Halfway to Heaven

There is a natural tendency to ignore, if not forget, the existing county boundaries that divide the Fens and, perhaps rightly, to think of the Fen country as a whole, as an independent kingdom in which three or four counties meet.

The Fens, by their very nature, have established their own boundaries which are marked by a change in the soil or a rise in the land. There are differences between the Fens of Cambridgeshire and those of South Lincolnshire, but they complement each other and no boundary commission or act of parliament can satisfactorily separate them more than the character of the people will allow.

The same can be said of Norfolk, which often gets overlooked as being part of the Fens, so rich is it in its other attractions. But who, I wonder, is consciously aware of being in either Cambridgeshire or Norfolk when travelling from Wisbech St Mary to West Walton, or from Manea to Nordelph. The Hundred Foot Washes from Mepal to Denver could not be more distinctly Fenland as they pass from one county to another, yet there is a subtle difference, both in the land and the dialect, and one needs to know these communities for a long time to recognize the individuality of each.

There is an even more pronounced difference when one moves further north into the Marshlands of Norfolk, renowned for their many fine churches. It is an area which has contributed greatly to the history of the Fen country and, for some people, often softens the otherwise bleak aspect of a land that is hard to understand at first or second sight. The Marshlands have also known the greed and ferocity of the sea when it breaks through the defences and seeks to reclaim what it has lost. No one can say that these normally quiet parishes are not an important chapter in fenland history.

As usual I did not approach my destination by the most direct route but sought the quieter roads from Little Downham-in-the-Isle, Pymoor, Hilgay and Ten Mile Bank to Denver. There was a reason for this as I wished to see for myself the 'country-heaven' remembered with such affection by another reader who wrote to me about his childhood in the Fens – Mr Leslie Scott, who was born in 1914 and knew the area intimately. Again, I can do no better than quote a few paragraphs from his interesting letters to illustrate the effect the place had on him all those years ago:

When I was a boy on our small farm at Pymoor and attending Pymoor School under the headship of Mr Smith, who later became Head of Coates School near Whittlesey, my parents felt the farm was too small to provide us all with a decent living and so I was sent to King's School, Ely, to prepare for something else. But I did work on the farm every holiday until I married at the age of 25. My boyhood saw me fishing in the local 'drains' or the big Hundred Foot, where one had to allow for a strong tide. When fishing in the drains, often near the Steam Engine Pumping Station, I first used to catch a smallish roach to which I'd fix a pike hook and hang this on a short line about a foot below a large float. This I then anchored to a long line about 20 yards away. While fishing for roach, tench or bream, I would keep an eye on the large float bobbing around and, if it made a sudden dart, I knew I'd got a pike. My mother used to cook eels and the coarse fish but never the pike which were so bony. I gave these to an aunt who was an expert at cooking them. She used to wash them well, soak them in very salty water overnight, then wrap them in bacon and cook ... James, the Fen Tiger, was much talked of with his prowess at catching eels and wildfowl. I also knew Will Kent who shepherded cattle on the Welney Washes, and Bailey Winters who shepherded the stretch between the railway line and Oxlode. They were great characters and both caught vast numbers of eels and wildfowl. Eel, duck and geese were regularly sent from Pymoor siding to London...

My mother was very strong Chapel and it was chapel three times each Sunday. Sunday School in the morning and then the adult services in the afternoon and evening. The Methodist Minister invariably came to our house for tea but when we all left for the evening service my father always managed to think up a reason for not going. He did attend Harvest Festivals but always looked uncomfortable in chapel. He was more comfortable and happy in a pub. In the 1920s my mother and I attended Oxlode Chapel which had its evening services from 6.00 p.m.–7 p.m. while Pymoor Church had its service from 6.30–7.30. As boys we used to leave Oxlode Chapel separately from our parents and on dark winter evenings, when we reached Pymoor, would find a cracked window and shine our torches into the rector's eyes, making him blink whilst he was still preaching. We thought this was great fun but did it once too often and were caught by the verger, who reported us to our mothers...

The name of our farm was Denmark Farm and the land ran down to the Hundred Foot Drain. My uncle and cousin farmed at Engine Farm, next to the Steam Engine Pumping Station, so I got to know the engineer there and my grandfather was also on the Ouse Drainage Board, so I learnt quite a bit about fen drainage. Another well-known man in the Fens at that time was Tom Mott who was a clever engineer as well as a good farmer. It was he who brought over from Germany a new machine for 'claying' the soil. This was a job which until then was done by hand. The men would dig trenches about 4–5 feet deep to reach the clay which they would then throw up left and right as far as they could. To have a machine that would do all this was a revelation...

You mentioned Christmas in one of your letters and we had much the same routine year after year. In my grandfather's time the family (two sons and two daughters with spouses and children – all boys) would meet at Denmark Farm for the usual Fen High Tea after which the men would be in one room playing cards for small stakes, and the women would be in another chatting. The boys would run around playing games, or roasting chestnuts on the open fires. Then late in the evening the ladies would prepare supper which always consisted of ham or pork with pickles, hot mashed potatoes and mushy peas. After supper the card-playing and whisky-drinking would continue into the small hours of the morning when the younger boys would be asleep. Then the aunts, uncles and cousins would depart, to get ready for the next day. Three more parties would follow in quick succession but Boxing Day was usually spent at my Uncle Harry's farm near Littleport when it was arranged that we should go hare-coursing or to a ploughing match...

My father was still cycling in the area when he was over eighty and was as stubborn as the best. Our farm house was on the same side of the road as the local small shop to which my father cycled whenever he wanted a new supply of 'baccy'. One day a police car stopped him and told him that he was cycling on the wrong side of the road. 'I know I am' he said sharply, 'but I don't reckon to cross the road and then have to come back again when both places are on the same side.' A few days later the police saw him again but threw up their hands in despair and drove on...

And I had to drive on from such remembered scenes if I was to get any further on my way. However, on Ten Mile Bank, I had to stop as I recalled one of my own memories. It was a late autumn Sunday afternoon and I was taking a coachload of visitors round the Fens. Twilight was already not far away. The sky had been full of magnificent clouds which were then deepening from creamy-white to desert-yellow and finally to an apricot-bronze. But a few miles before we reached Denver Sluice we found our way blocked by parked cars outside the small church just off the bank, where a harvest festival was being held. The place must have been packed and there was little we could do without disturbing the service. So we sat and waited. As the lusty strains of 'O Come all ye faithful' reached us the people in the coach started to join in and, as far as I can recall, no one grumbled, not even the coach driver. By the time we turned for home it was already dark.

The nearby rectory at Hilgay also has literary associations, not as well-known as those connected with Bluntisham and Christchurch. It was here that the poet, Phineas Fletcher, was rector from 1621–1650. He was born in 1582 and died when he was sixty-eight. His long narrative poem, *Britain's Ida*, was considered very erotic when it was published in 1628. His most popular and lasting work was *The Purple Island*, which appeared in 1633. He may be largely forgotten these days but unquestionably had a gift for a nicely turned phrase—

Love's tongue is in the eyes...

or, more provocatively,

Love is like linen often changed, the sweeter...

and surely the local landscape must have helped to inspire him when he wrote in one of his hymns—

In your deep floods / Drown all my faults and fears.

His brother, Giles Fletcher, was also a poet and the rector of Alderston in Suffolk. The dual role of priest and poet was not uncommon in the seventeenth century.

With my way to Denver unimpeded on that occasion I drove on into Marshland and to those villages where the Church clearly predominated over Chapel, for some of the finest buildings in the Fens are to be found in that Norfolk corner – Walpole St Peter, Terrington St Clement and West Walton among them.

Now that the harvest was over the fields looked more like empty rooms left unswept, the floorboards dusty from neglect and still awaiting new tenants. It would not take long. Another crop would soon be planted and the land expected to produce a few more tons of food. The earth gets little rest these days. Modern fertilizers revitalize it – at a price, and it is rare to see a fallow field (apart from 'set aside'). On the headlands the stacked bales of golden straw stood as solid as newly built cathedrals. Where the bales had not been piled up they lay about the fields more like druid stones, the ruins of a forgotten religion or the remains of a civilization that will be no more.

Across the land the silent and erect pylons were almost as symbolic, like bones picked clean, each one a skeleton haunting the distance. Motionless and gaunt, they stood as if time did not exist any more. Their purpose now was simply to measure space, to remind the future of an age that once saw itself as powerful and everlasting. But all our modern symbols of achievement will rust and fall into the shadows of our finished day. The old engineers that Mr Leslie Scott had written to me about would be amazed at the machines which, in less than a hundred years, had revolutionized farming.

But allow me for a moment to return to the subject of chapels because the growth of the Nonconformist movement in the Fens, particularly during the nineteenth century was phenomenal and there was a very strong division between Church and Chapel. It was political as much as religious. Church was Tory, Chapel Liberal (or Whigs) and Socialists were usually non-believers. When I first started writing about the Fens twenty-five years ago I would occasionally attend some of the Ebenezers, Bethesdas, Zion Tabernacles, the Baptists and Primitive Methodist chapels where, for generations loyal families had polished the pews with their Sunday-suited bottoms and had sung their favourite hymns. The preachers were often local men, popular in the area for their fiery sermons. Few of them used notes or were that well-read. They spoke, as they said, 'from the heart' or as they were 'guided by the holy spirit'.

It was in a chapel near Hilgay that I heard a sermon in which the preacher spoke to his congregation about the disciples:

> They were a rum lot to begin with. Unshaven and unkempt like some of you. They were mostly fishermen but could just as well have been ploughmen or horse-keepers. Nobody took much notice of 'em to begin with. If our Master were to come to the Fens today to look for his followers, who would he choose? Men like you, brothers. Charlie, there, and Tom, and you, Bert. Ordinary men of the soil. And what would the Church have to say to that? You don't need me to tell you for, as we all know, it is easier for a camel to pass through the eye of a needle than it is for a rich man to enter heaven. Can our present-day masters offer us heaven? If Hilgay was even half-way to heaven we'd never get there. But the day will come when the meek will inherit the earth...

Now most of those dreams and chapels are things of the past. The Victorian buildings, like so many of our village schools, have either been razed to the ground or converted into other uses. And I suppose that flashing a torch through a cracked window to annoy the vicar would be considered very tame mischief by today's boys.

So, have we gained, or lost? It is a question that every generation must have asked as it prepared to hand over to the future.

7 Talking About the Old Days

People are often puzzled when they come to the Fens for the first time and visit places such as Ramsey Heights or Gedney Hill. Where on earth are the hills? they ask. And so they might. Not that the names always mean what they imply but it is soon clear to them that there is nothing resembling a hill in the Fens. As a child I was equally baffled when my mother spoke of going up to the market hill to post a letter. Perhaps it was as a consolation that she always referred to going upstairs as 'up the wooden hill'. We had to imagine hills and mountains.

I was reminded of this as I made my way to Gedney Hill in the Lincolnshire Fens, where I was going to meet Mrs Constance Crouch and her husband Tom who, between them, could notch up over 160 years of experience in this unhilly country.

It was one of those afternoons that had about it a pleasant hint of melancholy which felt as if it could last forever. The fields, still empty for a brief rest after harvest, had the first bloom of autumn upon them. Isolated farmhouses appeared to be slowly sinking into the earth. Tall reeds in the dykes leaned towards the road which, after the dry summer, was deeply cracked and uneven. The village itself was as quiet as a siesta.

I found the bungalow, called Koroleigh, without any trouble and was warmly welcomed into the front room where Mrs Crouch was waiting to talk to me about her childhood in Parson Drove. She had already written out the answers to many of the questions I wanted to ask so I am able to let her tell her own story in her own words:

I was born on 2 February 1913 – Candlemas Day – at Parson Drove, near Wisbech. It was a rather large village

*'The Cage' – the village fire-engine station and
local 'lock-up'*

with its green surrounded by trees. Our house was one of a
row of various types of houses. The river-bank on the other
side of the road was the North Level Drain, known to us as
the Cut. Although my parents were not rich I had a happy
childhood.

When I was about three years old my father had to go
and serve in the First World War, mainly in Italy, and the
borders in the north. He didn't come home at all until the
Armistice and my mother and I had to stay at Parson
Drove by ourselves. There were many more women left
alone with their children. Not all saw their husbands
return. The house we lived in, like many others, has been
pulled down now and new ones built in its place.

I started school at the age of five. It was the old school,
which has also gone, just by the Swan public house. My

teacher's name was Miss Williams and the headmaster was a Mr L.T.D. Turner, a very stern man but greatly respected by us all.

In those days in a village everybody knew everybody else, not like today. When I went to school I had to pass the old building called 'The Cage' which housed the fire-engine which used to be pulled by horses when it was called to a fire. The water had to be pumped by men, who were all volunteers. I think at that time Mr Charles Garton was in charge as his blacksmith's shop was close by. There were some great old characters who used to sit by the forge fire talking about the old days. At the front of 'The Cage' was a clock, which was a memorial to Queen Victoria's Jubilee. Instead of numbers on its face for the hours it had twelve letters – V. R. SIXTY YEARS.

I can remember that on cold days I had a muff to keep my hands warm on the way to school and inside my muff my mother used to put a hot roasted potato, straight from the oven. Then, at break-time, I ate it for my lunch. It was cold by then, of course, but very different from the crisps and chocolates that children eat these days. We didn't have many playthings either but we were happy because everyone was the same and there were also some village highlights to amuse us on our way home from school. Sometimes we would see the travelling Pot Man who sold cups and saucers and all kinds of crockery. He used to set his wares out on the Green and we would hurry home to get our tea and then dash back for the sale, at which the village people would get stocked up for another year. Then there was the knife-grinder who came with his contraption which he peddled to turn the grinding-stone. Sometimes a small circus pitched their tents on the Green and that was always great fun.

Another event in those days was the annual dinner and shareout of the Sick and Dividend Club, which was held at the King William public-house in April. Huge joints of beef, steaming and hot, were loaded on to a lorry at Howard's bakehouse along the river-bank and pulled by men who brought it to the Foresters' Hall next to the pub, where the rest of the meal and the members of the club were waiting. In those days these benefit clubs were a great help to villagers as there was no Welfare State then to give them hand-outs. If the father of the family fell ill there were no wages, so the clubs helped to pay for medicines and doctors' bills. The more illness there was in a year the less money there was to divide out on the day.

There was another event known as Royal Oak Day

which was on 29 May, when we all wore a spray of oak
leaves in memory of King Charles II who, we were told,
had hid in an oak tree. The boys used to lay in wait for us
on our way to school and anyone caught not wearing an
oak spray was stung on the arms and legs with nettles...

Our summers were so colourful then with fields of
buttercups, cowslips, daisies, cuckoo-flower and yellow
irises, which we used to pick along Murrow bank. It was a
great strawberry growing area too and we used to get
holidays from school to help pick the strawberries and
other fruits. You could smell them for miles.

In the summer we had no fires in the grates with ovens
so we had a 'stew hole' in the wash-house and had all our
cakes and tarts cooked in the local bakehouses, one at
Howard's on the bank and one at Goodger's in Main Road.
Some people had their Sunday joints cooked there as
well...

Mrs Crouch's memories of those now distant days
continued with many more vivid and amusing recollections of the annual flower shows, the local dances, the
Sunday School anniversaries and festivals, when the
children rode round the village in farm wagons drawn by
heavy horses. Some of the children sang hymns whilst
others went from house to house collecting money. The
afternoon was passing all too quickly and there was still
much more to hear:

We didn't have our milk delivered in bottles or cartons in
those days but had to buy it from the farms. One of my
jobs before setting off for school was to fetch our milk in an
enamel can with a lid. We got our milk from Mrs Rowell at
Sycamore Farm. It meant getting up early and taking one
can for that day's milk and another empty can to be left for
the next day. Sometimes in the evenings we used to go to
another farm at Clough House to fetch cans of separated
milk that had had the cream taken from it for
butter-making. This milk was very frothy when it came out
of the separator and the cans had to have very tight lids.
Sometimes we used to swing the cans over and over above
our heads as we were walking home...

Mrs Crouch spoke repeatedly of the happiness and
contentment that her generation had known before she
left school at the age of fourteen. She told me that her
father was a shoemaker before moving to Sutton St

Edmund in 1927 to take over the village shop and post office. She was to work for him as his assistant for eight shillings a week and her keep. Her granddaughter asked her one day who bought her clothes. She smiled and said to me, 'They don't know they're born these days, do they!'

It was at Sutton St Edmund that she met the man who was to become her husband. Tom Crouch was a keen and talented athlete in his younger days – a champion runner, footballer and cricketer, 'but,' he said, 'there was no chance of being taken up and coached in those days if you were just an ordinary working person.'

I noticed from the clock on the mantelpiece that it was already close to half-past four and I had to prepare for leaving because of an evening engagement. It was not easy for Mrs Crouch produced a further bundle of notes and exercise-books telling the rest of her interesting story, holding in her arthritic hands a volume of local history that recorded many things that most people had forgotten and would never know again.

I expressed the wish that I would very much like to visit her again (which I was able to do a couple of weeks later) and that my departure was only a postponement of the next episode. After such a short time I felt I had known these good people all my life and had actually lived through the years that I had been hearing about. Mrs Crouch may have been forced to leave school at fourteen but her interests, her love of books, her powers of recall and her writing proved that, in a different age, she would have had many better opportunities. But I also realized that her story would then have been different too and I almost certainly would not have met her.

Before I left she flicked through the pages of an exercise-book in which she had recorded a list of the 154 tea-towels and more than 500 named carrier-bags from all over the world. 'I've never known a moment's boredom in all my life', she said. 'I've always had something to interest me, something to do. I can't stand idleness.'

As I drove away from the village the surrounding fields looked even more empty in the late afternoon light. The land-workers had gone home, the farm vehicles were silent. It was but a short-lived respite. Within a few days the farmers would be drilling, preparing for the next crops, for another year. In the distance I could see the reassuring shape of Crowland Abbey. Despite its troubled history it had a kind of permanence that we, as mortals, could never match. I always feel better when I see it, no matter how far away it is – and it can be seen for miles in the Lincolnshire Fens. There it was again, grey and solid, clinging like a barnacle to earth's hull. And no wind or wave would remove it – at least not in my lifetime.

8 A Plain, Straightforward Countryman

I shall never cease to be surprised at the number of coincidences in life (if that is what they are), nor at how frequently they occur in quick succession. Having written about Mrs Constance Crouch and her childhood in Parson Drove, I found myself just one week later, sitting in the drawing-room of the vicarage there, talking about someone else associated with the village in former days – Mr John Peck, who was born on 21 August 1787.

Having been told by my friend, the Reverend John Seaman, that John Peck had been actively involved in improving fen-drainage during the nineteenth century, that he had farmed and built in the area with great success, and also had a passion for hot-air balloons, my curiosity was easily kindled and I wanted to know more. So it was not long before I was invited over to Parson Drove to meet two ladies whose own lives seemed to have been taken over by a study of this extraordinary character who had kept a diary of life in the Fens for nearly forty years. Mrs Bridget Holmes was there as a relative of the Peck family, and Miss Dian Blawer as the transcriber of the closely handwritten diary. Both had already done an enormous amount of research and had recently mounted an exhibition in Wisbech Museum to draw attention to John Peck's achievements. I was impressed by their dedication and enthusiasm.

But, I wondered, would I be able to work their knowledge into a chapter for this book? And how would I react to the suggestion that this relatively unknown fenman's diary could even be compared with the more famous one kept by the Reverend Francis Kilvert? It was, admittedly, a cautious claim but if it were true then, surely, here was a discovery indeed.

It was a lovely early autumn day and the high room was filled with mellow sunlight. After the recent torrential rain and thunderstorms which had brought the long hot summer to a sudden end, it was a comfort to feel that a restful calm had returned to the English seasons. In this tranquil atmosphere various episodes in John Peck's life began to fall casually as yellow leaves from earth's own pages.

John was proud of his farming ancestry and his country, seeing himself as a yeoman rather than a gentleman farmer. When his father died in 1812 he became head of the family, responsible for his widowed mother and the younger children. He was twenty-five and then living at Parson Drove, having moved from his native village of Newton four years earlier. Soon he was farming four hundred acres on land divided between Parson Drove, Tydd Fen and Sutton St Edmund. This gave him the added advantage of three votes at election time. To begin with he saw himself mainly as a grazier, breeding sheep, cattle and pigs, but with his land around Parson Drove and Throckenholt being better suited to arable crops – wheat, oats, barley, potatoes and turnips, his farming activities expanded. It was not an easy time for a young farmer with ambitions. Agriculture was in a deep depression, the economy was poor, there were corn riots over prices and wages, and many of the problems of fen drainage were still to be solved. To make matters worse the Government's Free Trade policy meant that the home markets were soon over-supplied by imports from other countries and locally grown products were not wanted. It sounds a familiar story even though it is 180 years old.

In 1817 John Peck, at the age of thirty, married Elizabeth Ulyatt, the daughter of a neighbouring farmer. As well as taking an interest in her husband's career she also bore him seven sons and one daughter, all of whom prospered. The eldest son followed his father into farming and became the master brewer of Parson Drove Brewery. The third son emigrated to Australia where he made and then lost a fortune, but lived to become a prominent citizen of Melbourne, where he died at the age of eighty.

In addition to being a farmer and vigorous campaigner

A silhouette of Mr John Peck

for better drainage in the Fens, John Peck was also Constable of Parson Drove from 1816 to 1851; the local tax assessor and valuer; an arbitrator in local dispute; a talented cricketer; and an expert ice-skater. He was no mean draughtsman and made many sketches of houses in the village, and also arranged for Parson Drove to have its own fire engine – the one housed in 'The Cage' spoken of in the previous chapter by Mrs Crouch.

Tempting as it is, this chapter is not meant to be a biography of such a fascinating and energetic fenman. That task belongs to someone else and deserves more than a few thousand words. My purpose is simply to illustrate what a good diarist he was and to support the idea of forming a John Peck Society. If he turns out to be the Fens' own Francis Kilvert that will be all to the good. His diary certainly covers a longer period of history than Kilvert's (who died when he was only thirty-nine) and records an earlier era. John Peck was writing at a time of turbulent change, from Waterloo to the Industrial Revolution and the Great Exhibition of 1851, which he visited shortly before he died in the autumn of that year.

As with all diaries there are many entries which are about the ordinary, often trivial day-to-day things that happen in a family – children's illnesses, birthdays, dinner-parties; but there are also those entries which give us a wonderful insight into what life was like in the Fens during the first half of that vibrant century. When he is not being just factual his descriptions can be as evocative as Dorothy Wordsworth's, whose Journal I was reminded of perhaps more than Kilvert's. Take this example from an entry in January 1834:

A soft wind blowing from the south and the sun quite warm. Flowers are springing up and the birds singing. Walked to Tydd Fen in the morning; in the afternoon round the home fields; grass and all looking flourishing ... Weather continues bright and fine ... May flowers are budding. Old folk say 'We must have a pincher at Spring' and many a more similar sayings ... How ever the spring may be I always rejoice to get the dull and dreary short days over with ... A January like this but few remember.

Such an entry contradicts the beliefs that years ago the winters were always hard, with plenty of frost or snow. It reminded me of a similar entry in John Clare's journal of ten years earlier where, on Christmas Day 1824, he wrote: 'Gathered a handful of daiseys in full bloom; saw woodbine & dogrose in the woods putting out in full leaf & a primrose root full of ripe flowers.'

Let me offer a few of John Peck's other entries by putting them in chronological order:

14.4.21.   At Wisbech, business completely at a stand and poor farmers looking each other in the face as much as to say, 'What's the matter?' The times are fearful; God only can know the end.

8.12.21.   At Wisbech the market in a wretched state; not one merchant came into the Corn Exchange. Wheat as low as 20/- per quarter, oats £4 per last. Farmers standing looking at each other in astonishment, exclaiming that something must be done.

17.3.27.   At Wisbech the wind rough and stormy, which in the afternoon increased to a hurricane, tearing the canvas off the booths. Went to the Angel and saw the French Giant, 7 ft. 6 in. high. I could but look at my own insignificance.

A later entry that year, on 21 November, was of particular interest because of a reference to John Clare. John Peck, whose favourite poet was Lord Byron, clearly kept up to date with new publications of what was then 'modern' poetry. Clare's *The Shepherd's Calendar* was published in April 1827. Mr Peck may not have been over-enthusiastic about the Helpston poet's most ambitious work, which he considered 'fair', but he did admire one of Clare's sonnets which appeared eight years later in *The Rural Muse* and copied it out on the back of the title page:

> Old stone pits with veined ivy overhung;
> Wild crooked brooks o'er which is rudely flung
> A rail and plank that bends beneath the tread ...

This would have been a familiar experience to any countryman at that time, especially in the Fens where the dykes were often crossed on narrow planks. So too would have been the poet's description of the church steeple 'peeping and stretching in the distant sky'.

An entry on 3 March 1829 shows that it is not only today's children who have a relish for horror:

> Wisbech Mart. Very many shows and much idle company. Bought rock for the children, a pleasant sweet now much in fashion ... Took the two eldest boys to see several shows. Among the peep-shows the great attraction was the murder of Maria Martin in the Red Barn, with the execution of Corder. The boys seemed satisfied, and I really think they were, for I can remember the pleasure such things gave me as a child.

Several entries in 1831–2 then reveal the seriousness of another horror – cholera, which was having a devastating effect on the population of the Fens as elsewhere. Month by month John Peck recorded its spread through Europe and then East Anglia:

> 29.6.31. The cholera morbus, a dreadful disease, is now ravaging the north of Europe and great fears are entertained it may be introduced into England ...

Those fears were soon realized and John Peck wrote in November of that year of a ship from Sunderland, loaded with coals, sailing into Wisbech where it was placed in quarantine, 'hoisting a Yellow Flag in the day, with a candle and lanthorn at her masthead in the night'. In the following March he added:

> The cholera having made its appearance at Ely, the Chief Justice deemed it proper to hold the Assizes at this town instead. The east end of Ely lies very low, inhabited almost entirely by poor persons, and is extremely filthy ... the higher portion of the city, richer and cleaner, is entirely free at present.

By the June of 1832 it had reached Guyhirn where a stout old man who was quite fit in the morning, died ten hours later. The Towns of March and Whittlesey were among those badly affected and 'many are dying daily'. In July we read:

> The cholera has made some progress in the neighbour-hood. Every person you meet from another village asks with alarm how you are at home. Burning the beds and clothes of persons who have died is now adopted and, by order of the Privy Council, burial grounds remote from the towns are to be provided.

When the epidemic was finally over the diary entries return to more domestic and local affairs. In the farming world the weather is not just a subject for idle gossip, it affects life and has its own drama. The end of August 1833 saw a great storm which John Peck recorded in detail:

> 31.8.33.   Yesterday we had to fetch water in tubs to wet the straw, this morning the yards are 6 inches deep, such a very heavy rain fell in the night, with a very high wind ... As the day got up the storm began to increase until it blew a perfect hurriance, with torrents of rain which continued all day. So wretched a one I never can remember at this season of the year. The wet and cold were so intense, hundreds of sparrows and small birds have been picked up dead ...

That word 'hurriance' is not a mis-spelling of hurricane, it was a word often used by the diarist to describe that kind of stormy weather. The wind continued the following day 'to blow with great violence', with 'trees torn up by their roots'.

The mild winter of 1834, which I referred to earlier, obviously continued for a few more weeks for John Peck tells us that the February days remained hot and that he was able to 'cut some summer cauliflowers for dinner'. A butterfly also came into the house and a sparrow's nest with two eggs was found under the eaves of a stack. In August 1835, he gave us a particularly vivid description of what the landscape was like:

> Grass fields like to mahogany, and the sheep drove (by the shepherds) up to the river for water, which I never knew before. This has been a searing week, water all gone, grass also ... No water for the cattle but what is got from the New Drain – and thank God it is there for us to get.

Before concluding this introduction to an extraordinary fenman, whom the Reverend Frederic Jackson was to describe as 'a plain, straightforward countryman', I must make further reference to his love of flight which, in his day, was manifesting its wonders in hot-air ballooning. In 1826 he had copied out from *Blackwood's Magazine*: 'Why do we think it a glorious thing to fly? Because our feet are bound to the dust. We enjoy the eagle's flight far more than the eagle himself, for Imagination dallies with an unknown power and the wings that are denied to our bodies expand our souls.'

John Peck travelled miles to see air balloons. Sometimes he only had to step outside his back door. On 19 August 1823 he records that 'fifteen minutes to 8 o'clock in the evening a balloon descended near our house. It was launched from near Abingdon in Berkshire at five minutes before 6 o'clock; a distance of about 100 miles.' Then, on 2 July 1825 a balloon from Stamford landed near Thorney. 'To the people of Parson Drove it was in view more than half an hour ... and many rode and ran to see the wonder.' A year later he rode to Boston to see an ascent and even offered the aeronaut £5 to take him up with him. For the next twenty years he continued to make entries about these 'magnificent balloons' but never achieved making a flight himself. His grandson in Australia did learn to fly an aeroplane and passed his qualifying test, but he himself was refused a pilot's licence on account of his age. He was eighty-one.

Hot-air balloon rising from the Fens

And so the active and adventurous life of John Peck
went on until 1851 when he was suddenly taken ill and
died on 18 October. He thought his brief illness was due to
tiredness after a strenuous harvest and that his cough was
caused by getting soaked in the fields. But at sixty-four his
heart was already weak and within twenty-four hours of
paying his men their wages on Saturday, he collapsed. At
his request his faithful labourers bore his coffin to the
church on one of his own waggons. The road was lined
with sorrowing villagers and every pew in St John's
Church filled with those who had managed to get into the
service, where the Reverend Frederic Jackson gave his
moving tribute to a man whose deeds were his
monument. (St John's Church was closed in 1973 and the

Church of Emmanuel, nearer to the village green, became the parish church.) At least John Peck had made the most of his last summer, spending three days in July at the Great Exhibition in Hyde Park, where all was wonder. 'Spent seven hours in viewing the ground floor only. Head dizzy with so many grand things which I had not the least conception of.' He visited the theatre and art galleries where 'the sculpture pleased me' and 'the diamonds astonished me'. There was music and fireworks in profusion and he could hardly believe that such things existed. He looked forward to the future with equal excitement.

Little wonder to me that Bridget Holmes, Dian Blawer and John Seaman would like to perpetuate this man's achievements by forming a John Peck Society. But for their efforts those rich accounts of life in the nineteenth century would have slept in darkness for much longer. Safe, but unread. If their dreams materialize we shall all be able to share more fully in the memories of an outstanding man. It is not too late for him to inspire others.

9   The Indescribable Joys

The next episode in my sequence of coincidences came within hours of hearing about the life of John Peck and, again, it concerned the village of Parson Drove.

This time I was to meet the man who became the subject of the present chapter – Mr Alwyn Johnson, a working farmer who rightly takes pride in never having lived more than 300 yards from where he was born, even though he has moved house six times.

I was soon to realize that, far from being parochial, in the narrow sense of the word, he had as many interests as any world traveller. He has been a member of the National Trust for more than twenty-five years; still works on a voluntary basis for the British Trust for Ornithology; loves reading – especially books on archaeology, local history and ancient buildings; and has played in a brass band for most of his life. He was also churchwarden of St John's Church until it closed in 1973; has served on the local drainage board, and, in addition, carried on the farming traditions that were started by his family eight generations ago. This list by no means exhausts his interests.

The family already has a small claim to immortality in the Fens because Johnson's Drove was named after it and there are references to it on early fenland maps. Alwyn's forefathers would have known the Fens before they were drained and each generation has been witness to the many dramatic changes that have taken place during the past three or four hundred years. So when he took me out to one of the first fields they had owned all those years back I knew I was in the presence of a man who had every right to call himself a fenman. He also has the features and the pale blue eyes of a fenman, though is considerably taller than most. I couldn't help thinking that in his hey-day he might have been a match for the fenland giant, Tom Hickathrift.

Alwyn was born in 1926 and, like his two brothers and his parents, went to the local village school. The house where he was born – Woad Mill Farm house – speaks of its own history when woad was grown in large quantities in the Fens.

I had met him on two previous occasions but then invited myself to his house so that we could have a longer chat. Before settling down for that I asked if we could go out to see the fields he still farmed. He willingly agreed and we got into his truck to drive off through the village. 'Parson Drove', he said, 'is as typical a fen-village as you could find these days. We have a good community here that helps to keep the old traditions alive.'

He began to point to different buildings. 'That's where my parents once lived … that's where John Peck's house was … that wall there was built by his son … and there's the 'Cage' … Now we're going to cross over the New Cut…'

We came to the cross-roads and I saw the tiny square building that John Peck had built for the fire-engine and as a lock-up for local offenders. On our right-hand side was the war memorial. When I looked at it later I noticed that the village lost more men in the Second World War than it did in the First, and that six of those young men, all in their twenties, had died in Japanese prisoner-of-war camps. They were a few of the many men in the 2nd Cambridgeshire Regiment who were to die in the Far East, mostly from starvation and brutality.

A moment or two later we had crossed the main road and were bumping down a green drove where not many folk were allowed to go, and when Alwyn got out of his truck to unlock a gate in the middle of nowhere, I knew I was receiving a special privilege.

'That's Throckenholt over there,' he said. 'It was originally called Everderwide, then Trockenholt. I've no idea when they put the "h" in. It was once the site of an hermitage given to the monks of Thorney Abbey as a retreat by Nigellus, Bishop of Ely during the reign of Henry II. Then in 1540 it became a chapel.'

As if the date was significant he pointed to a twelve-acre field on my left. 'That's where we started, or perhaps I

should say, that's one of the earliest fields we have
documents for. I know we've been farming here for more
than eight generations but we could go back further. It's
still a good feeling.'

In the distance, about eight miles away as the crow flies,
we could see the smoking brickyard chimneys at King's
Dyke, Whittlesey, and Yaxley. Around us the fields were
full of lapwings arriving for their winter feeding-grounds.
A little further away was a heronry and Alwyn told me
about the bird-counts he did for the British Trust for
Ornithology, mainly herons and barn-owls, which, like
the skylarks, are getting fewer and fewer because there is
nowhere safe for them to nest.

'The land was never as open as this, not even when I
was a boy,' he explained.

There used to be plenty of thorn hedges and gates then.
Every field was enclosed, which was useful when the land
was put out for grazing. Years ago the Fens around Parson
Drove were mostly for cattle and sheep. That was when
the wealth was in wool. Farmers bred sheep then mainly
for the fleece, like they did in Norfolk. There was very little
arable land. Now it's just the opposite – little grazing and
nearly all arable. It's all to do with money in the end. I can
remember in 1948 you'd have four men working for every
one hundred acres. Now you'll find only two men working
how many hundred acres? Six hundred? Often more.
When I started working on the farm it was very
labour-intensive, especially at harvest or crop-lifting. It was
always a pleasure to go to work then because you were
working all day with men who could laugh and talk about
ordinary village happenings, day after day, joking with
each other until it was time to go home. Men used to
whistle a lot in them days. You hardly ever hear that now.
It's more likely to be Radio 1. Today, farming's a very
lonely occupation, with machines doing most of the work.
I've spent days out here on my tractor without seeing or
speaking to a soul. I can understand why some men need a
cab radio.

When we turned into Johnson's Drove Alwyn was able
to show me the house where his greatgrandfather had
lived.

The drove was not made up like it is today and when he died the weather had made the track too muddy to get the funeral carriages down. So they had to carry his body across those two fields to get to the main road. The first field belonged to my greatgrandfather, but the second one belonged to a Mr Egar who would only agree to the body crossing his land if our family signed an agreement to say it did not constitute a right of way – which is how many of the old rights of way came into existence.

I tried to imagine how this long-distant shot would look on film in some period drama and, for those few seconds, enjoyed a journey back in time.

An hour later we returned to the house for a cup of tea and I asked Alwyn to tell me more about his childhood.

Well, I can remember when I was only five years old I was given my first bicycle to help me to get to school on time. And we played all the usual games of course – whip-and-top, hoops, conkers, dyke-jumping and swimming. Later I played football for the school as their goal-keeper but I can't have been very successful 'cus I was substituted in the second-half. When I was older I pulled in Gorefield's tug-o'-war team and won several trophies at that.

He took one off the sideboard shelf to show me.

From the age of ten he was expected to do his share of work on the farm. He was taught how to milk the cows, feed the bullocks, ducks, pigs, chickens and geese, how to look after the horses and drive the herds out for grazing. As a boy he also kept rabbits and ferrets, and learnt from his grandfather how to handle two horses and the harrows. 'There was always plenty to do,' he said, 'and I have to say that I had a very happy childhood. I thought it would never end. The days were never long enough.'

He spoke too of the fun they had at home on Saturday nights making toffee and how, once a week, they had a special treat of a ¼ lb of chocolate-drops. 'Simple pleasures that they wouldn't say thank-you for today. They soon won't even know what a ¼ lb is, will they!?'

We then returned to the subject of farming and I heard how, during the war years, many of the new tractors came over from America under the lend-lease programme. 'Most of the tractors had the Stars and Stripes painted all over them,' said Alwyn, 'which seemed a bit strange to me on an English farm.'

There weren't always enough tractors to go round and so those farmers with a Ministry of Agriculture card used to go along to the sales where they would put their cards into a bag – a bit like a raffle – and the ones whose names were drawn out bought the tractors. It was to stop any bribing going on, I suppose. I can tell you this, that in all that time our card was never once pulled out of the bag. But we got by. Sometimes if things got a bit hard we would thresh a bit more corn for the market. But you'd never let on that's what you were doing. If anyone asked you always said you were just threshing for a bit of straw or chaff for the stock. Once a year, usually on Boxing Day, we would turn over the faggot-stack. This was the stack we had built mainly out of sticks and hedge-cuttings. During the winter months the rabbits would burrow under there to keep warm and, naturally, they multiplied so quickly that something had to be done to keep down the population. So with a horse and some ropes we'd turn the stack over and put our spades over the warren-holes, then as we drove the rabbits out we'd catch them and break their necks. Shooting was out of the question because of the other animals. Most of the rabbits were given away to our neighbours who, even at Christmas, could do with a bit extra to eat. Now we all have too much, don't we.

I put it to Alwyn that he had obviously got as much pleasure out of farming as he had out of his childhood. 'It's been wonderful,' he said.

It's always struck me that there can be few jobs where you can get a greater sense of fulfilment. From ploughing to harrowing, from drilling to harvesting, you can always see the results of your labours. You don't always get your own way, nature sees to that. But that's only a challenge, not a disaster. The joys and pleasures of farming make up for all that. They are just indescribable. I have been a very happy man and would like to believe that I have done no harm to anybody. My grandfather used to say that 'honesty is the only word you need to live by' and I think that putting that into practice has enabled me to go to bed every night with an easy conscience. You've got to be true to what you know is right, for others as well as yourself. I've never known a dishonest person who was truly happy.

I then asked him how he would describe the character of the fenman.

'Well, that's a difficult thing to say in a sentence, but let me put it like this – you can lead a fenman with a piece of string but there's never been a stick big enough to drive him. He knows his own mind and who his friends are.'

'That seems to sum him up perfectly,' I said.

If the days had never been long enough for Alwyn Johnson, the afternoon had certainly not been long enough for me. Talking with a man who has known nothing but fen life, who has worked with horses, reapers and binders, as well as the latest machines to be used on the land, gives one a genuine insight into the history and traditions of a place. And, as he pointed out, he was but a link between the past and the future, for he has a son and a grandson for whom the land will no doubt mean as much.

What had struck me about this man on each of the occasions we had met was his constant happiness. Smiles and laughter were never far away and he still takes pleasure in all that he does, whether it is farming, reading, bird-watching, playing in a brass band, helping to run a garden fete, or showing someone like me around his own part of the Fens. Because he has kept his mind so active his memories are many and varied. As he reeled off a number of anecdotes about local characters of the past he could hardly finish them for laughing – Bill Townsend, who was famous for his potent homemade mushroom ketchup, which he served with everything; Frank Fuller, a gentleman of the road, who made a winter home for himself in a deserted seed-shop now completely covered in ivy; men who could drink twenty pints of mild ale in an evening and then go home and have a bowl of hot mutton fat for supper. 'They were,' said Alwyn, 'men of considerable constitution.'

He then returned to the sideboard and took down another trophy of which he was unashamedly proud, not only for himself but for his village. It was when their brass band became the Triple Prize-winners of East Anglia at Norwich in 1958, taking the President's coveted trophy for scoring the highest number of points in the day's events. 'And there were some good bands there that day, too.'

After such an encounter with a fenman of Mr Johnson's

stature and experience, I find it difficult to concentrate on my driving as I make my way home. Fortunately I know all the narrow, bumpy back-roads and do not have to compete with the heavier traffic on the A47. But on that day I would have been grateful for a chauffeur so that I could savour the memory of all that had been said. As I have never relied on tape-recorders, or whatever latest gadgets are used, I need to get pen to paper fairly quickly. In that way I like to believe that I am recalling a conversation rather than an interview. So, on my journey back to reality, I was able to visualize the funeral cortège of Alwyn's greatgrandfather as his coffin was carried across the winter fields for burial; I could see the schoolboys dyke-jumping and hear the rattle of hoops on the road; I could even hear the men on the land, laughing as they worked, their songs and jokes forever lost now under a pensive sky. If I have caught something of that vanished world, I am both vindicated and pleased.

When I began this book I had no idea that the little village of Parson Drove would provide me with three of these chapters, or that I would meet such generous

Something of that vanished world

people, willing to share their memories with me. But, as I am sure I have said before, the Fens never cease to surprise. Because they do, they constantly enrich and make me even more grateful for their existence.

10   Farewell, Mr Thorney

When a king dies, a nation mourns. Is any man's death less than a king's? Each man has his own people, and his house is his kingdom. Each day, in villages and towns, a king dies. Neighbours and friends gather to shed their tears and remember. More often than not they come, not out of loyalty, but of love. Sorrow moves people in various ways.

For a couple of weeks during the hot summer of which I write, my wife and I went walking in the Austrian Alps. One day, in the village of Lannersbach, we watched the funeral of a local resident who was also a fireman. Obviously he was greatly respected. His colleagues were there to honour him, dressed in their uniforms and bright shining helmets. Members of the local brass band played beautifully outside the church as the ornate coffin was wheeled into the cemetery. The sound was rich and mellow, as if they wanted to create the ideal elegy for his passing. Flags were lowered and the villagers filed past to pay their own silent homage. He could have been a king. For those who mourned, perhaps, he was.

We had heard the bell tolling as we came down the hill. There are few more evocative sounds of sadness than the mournful ringing of a funeral bell. The only sound that I find always surpasses it is the playing of the saddest music of all – *The Last Post*.

By the time we reached the church the service was almost over and the mourners had moved into the orderly cemetery with its wrought-iron crosses and flowered graves. The afternoon was golden and still. And, a village surrounded by mountains and pine forests can be very still indeed.

I have often thought that one is more rudely aware in

the mountains of man's mortality than in somewhere like the Fens. Mountains can be so awesome in their solid weight and sense of permanence. They have been there, almost, from the beginning, and always look as if they will last until eternity. Beside such impressive monuments of nature, human beings are made to look insignificant, a mere incident in the strange patterns of creation. Our brief span of life seems almost as short as that of the millions of insects that crawl over every inch of the mountain-sides. Even the small shrines and home-made crosses along the *wanderwegs* serve as reminders that we are not here for long, so let's make the most of it.

But, in the Fens, it feels different for they are, after all, man-made territories and may even disappear within the lifetime of a younger generation. The Fens were not always there and something else made by man must inevitably take their place. It is because I have always been aware of such great space, such limitless distance and light, that I have been helped in my coming to terms with both mortality and eternity. A person can feel small in the Fens, but can also feel strangely uplifted and important – an integral part of nature rather than its subject. And so the funeral in an Austrian village became even more poignant and relevant because of what was to happen later. The strands of the web were being drawn together.

I was to be reminded of that particular moment of our sunlit summer just a few days after we had returned home for, whilst we were away, my dear friend Hugh Cave, had died at the age of ninety-two. Fortunately we were back in time to attend his funeral, at which I had promised to read a poem specially written for the occasion. That promise had been made nine or ten years earlier and my tribute was already written, mainly because Hugh wanted to see it before he died. I told him then that it was a premature request but would see what I could do.

I had known Hugh personally for twenty-five years, from the day he knocked at my door wanting at least six copies of my first book – *Portrait of the Fen Country* signed as Christmas presents. His second wife, Renate, who came from Hamburg, was with him and immediately I sensed that an important friendship was in the making. So it turned out to be. He was a wonderful source of local and fenland knowledge and was to feature in five of my later books. We spent hours in each other's company and were never at a loss for something to talk about. There were times when I went for morning coffee and stayed long enough to hear the neighbouring abbey clock chime midnight.

Hugh had a zest for living that was inspirational, even when on his fourth pace-maker. He had even made plans for the celebration of his hundredth birthday. Always active in the community, he made sure that Thorney's history was preserved for all to share in the future. He was a man of wisdom and laughter, of mischief and seriousness, always enjoying a serious discussion as well as a joke. He was never bored and, therefore, never boring. Local builder, councillor, historian and Justice of the Peace – no wonder he was called 'Mr Thorney'. On the day that the village mourned his passing, could anyone deny that he was anything less than a king who had served his people well for nearly a hundred years?

So, at what turned out to be the end of an idyllic summer, we gathered in Thorney to say thanks and farewell to a very special man. It was as if he had carefully stagemanaged his own funeral. The morning began with torrential rain and hovering clouds which threatened more. It was already beginning to look like a scene from a Thomas Hardy novel. Why is it, in fiction and in films, nearly all funerals are conducted in the pouring rain, especially when it is to be burial, as this one was? All it required were horses with black plumes and a brass band playing an arrangement of Chopin's funeral march.

The service was held in the abbey church and the noisy rooks were already lamenting above the churchyard trees as if they had been appointed as nature's professional mourners. Inside the abbey the pews gradually filled with neighbours and friends as the organist played *Pie Jesu* from Faure's *Requiem*. This was also a rare, if not unique, occasion because Hugh was a lifelong Roman Catholic who wanted his funeral service in the local Anglican church which, as an historian, he had loved all his life. It was an appropriate bringing together of several faiths I believe, as well as acquaintances. Could anyone imagine Hugh's funeral being anywhere else? So he had his Requiem Mass in the building that he loved, and the village for an hour stood still. After Communion I was asked to read the poem I had written for him several years before and was struck by how accurate my description of the day turned out to be, and even more so the burial. I had called my poem *Before an Obituary*. Now it was both that and something more.

> When you die it will be
> More than the death of a man
> Or the fall of a tree.
> More than a village will mourn,
> More than a house feel some branch crack
> When your leaves drop from the sombre sky.
>
> When light breaks down
> In the heart of the sun
> And silence broods alone in the dark,
> More than a friend will have gone
> From rooms we never thought would share,
> The stark cold stare of the grieving rain.
>
> But, never so soon that we
> Must shed our tears before
> That cortège of clouds moves over the Green.
> Keep back the years that we might say
> 'We knew a man who was centuries wise,
> As firm as a rock, as fine as a tree'.
>
> Then, when that morning comes
> Without your greeting at the door,
> We shall be proud to claim
> A branch of kinship with your name,
> To feel, like roots that never lose their grip,
> The still warm, lasting shake of your hand.

Shortly afterwards we made our way to the village cemetery for the interment and the first thing I noticed was that Hugh's grave, most fittingly, was under a mighty oak tree. In a strange way I then felt that I had not written those lines but that they had been given to me for this occasion.

As we walked back to the house the rain ceased and a few frail beams of sunlight reminded us of what the summer had been like. And then the dark clouds returned and we drove home. Perhaps, after all, we had been reminded of man's mortality, even in the Fens. We can't escape it wherever we live.

What I do know is that the Fens have meant more to me because I had the good fortune to meet a man like Hugh, a man who could be a stern critic of anything I said which did not please him but who never failed to encourage me to write about the places and the people we both so greatly admired. Some of his last words to me were 'Edward, so many people have been good to me that I want them all to know how grateful I have been. I have had a fortunate life. Do tell them I was grateful. Do keep writing about them, and the Fens.'

Extremes are often linked together by coincidences and my mountain walks of that glorious year will forever be associated with the departure of 'Mr Thorney', a real pace-setter. And whenever I visit his grave I am sure my memory will also connect with the funeral of the Austrian fireman, so that a stranger and a friend become, as it were, companions of an experience. That walk will have engraved itself on to my map of the Fens and I shall see the glint of sunlight on brass helmets as I watch each year's new acorns swelling on the oak tree giving shade to a wonderful character. There will never be another 'Mr Thorney' but we shall never be without him either for he has already become a legend. The last thing I said to Hugh before going on holiday was 'don't worry, I shall soon be back to pick your brains'. He tried to reply but neither I nor his wife Renate could quite understand what he said. I think I shall always find it difficult to write a book without him in it somewhere and I am indebted to his family for allowing me to use that sad occasion as a tribute in this volume.

11 That Place, Those Hours

The street where I was born was a village within a town and I can never walk down it now without seeing it as it was then, more than sixty years ago.

The houses that have replaced the ones I knew are, of course, better in many ways, with more spacious rooms, more indoor facilities, electric lights, central heating and bathrooms; none of which we had. Most of them now even have attractive front gardens and those that still remain from an earlier history have been improved almost beyond recognition. Even the shops and pubs have been converted into private homes and it must be difficult for today's residents to imagine what it was like when life for everyone was so very different.

But, the moment I step into Church Street, I experience something like a Resurrection Day. All is restored. In the twinkling of an eye, all is changed. The old terraced houses are back, the sounds, smells, names and neighbours I knew as a boy, return to take their places in a scene that, for me, can never disappear – the Ashbys, Coles, Clarkes, Holmans, Chamberlains, Papworths, Redheads, Claypoles, Drivers, Goodwins, Blakes, Whiteheads, Avelings and Shaws; the rag-and-bone man, the cobbler, milkman, carpenter, grocers, butchers and coalman; the fish-and-chip shop, the publicans and vicar; the potato merchant, the bus garage, the chapel, the Salvation Army hall and the church; the farm-workers, tradesmen and brickyard workers, all living cheek by jowl in a world that was as independent as any world could be.

I look at it now, not with nostalgia but with affection, because it became part of me, and is still with me, unchanged, richer and more loveable because of experience, because of the Now which is living my present life and will, one day, itself become Past. And the past is not necessarily dead, or a condition to be avoided. It can't be. It has to be understood and made use of, with regret, or gratitude. We simply have to make the most of what it gave us, not by trying to re-live *it* but by allowing it to live again in us, with a more perceptive eye than childhood can offer.

That street was the cauldron, making and shaping us into the individuals we were to become. Some, naturally, changed more than others. One or two boys went to the grammar schools in March or Peterborough and the rest of us went to the local C. of E. Boys School. Some went to work in the brickyards and one or two went to university. Some became tradesmen and others worked on the land. One became a priest, another became a poet. There were jealousies, arguments, falling-outs and making-ups; there was snobbery and disenchantment, covetousness and pride; but there was also kindness and love, respect and a willingness to help. All these factors resolved themselves in the warm spirit of humanity which, in such tightly knit communities, knows how to forgive, to laugh and to accept, if it is to survive. Neighbours helped each other and frequently the better-off gave practical assistance to those less fortunate, without making a great noise about it. It was often years later than one learned of a generous deed or an interest-free loan. The street contained all shades of society and, although not feudal, knew where the barriers must not be crossed. From the Packhorse Inn at one end to the Boat Inn at the other, was a microcosm of humankind.

For the first few years our immediate neighbours were the Porters at No. 15 and the Staffords at No. 19 but eventually they moved into other parts of the town – which was tantamount to going abroad – and their places were taken by the Papworths and the Redheads, whose children grew up with me and some of whom I still meet on occasions to talk about an age that undoubtedly ended with the Second World War. I mention those families because one in particular will take some prominence as this chapter develops. But, for a moment, I will stay with the street itself, for it was to be my world for the first twenty-five years of my life and the place I most clearly associate with childhood.

As I explained in my book *Fen Boy First* there was seldom any need to go beyond that street into any other part of the town because it was so self-sufficient and could have withstood a siege. Even when I started school I only had to turn into Thoroughfare Lane (between Turners and Wintertons the butchers) to approach the infants and junior schools by the back door. Both attempted to provide the basic educational requirements of that pre-Butler era and even when I went up to the Senior Boys School in Station Road, half of my classes were held in the Methodist Chapel schoolroom just a few doors away from our house. So the only real 'beyond' was that open paradise which awaited me once I had passed St Andrew's Church and crossed Briggate Bridge on my way to Blackbush or Ramsey Road to gather dandelions for my rabbits.

Whatever time of day or season of the year it is when I return now it simply becomes the equivalent of what it was then. I see the boys playing marbles or fag-cards; the girls playing hop-scotch or hoop-racing; or all of us playing whip-'n'-top or hide-and-seek. In one house I can still hear a boy practising his cornet; in another someone learning the violin. From the steps of the chapel newly made model aeroplanes are launched on their brief flights to the other side of the road, or a small huddle of boys are trying out a new burning-glass beneath the mid-day sun, scorching holes through pieces of paper or singeing the backs of their hands in some mild game of torture. From what was the taproom of the White Horse pub I can hear the shuffle of dominoes or the muted thud of darts into a board. A few steps further on I stand outside the Salvation Army hall and listen to the prayer-meeting being held inside. The same earnest pleas, the same chorus, as if it had been going on unceasingly for sixty years:

> I need Thee, oh I need Thee,
> Every hour I need Thee.
> Oh bless me now my Saviour,
> I come to Thee.

Religion and politics were an inevitable part of the street's life, like funerals, weddings, fights, tea-parties and babies. We had Conservatives, Liberals and Socialists, just as we had Anglicans, Non-conformists, Roman Catholics

and atheists. Children who did not go to Sunday School
would stand outside on Sunday mornings and mock the
choruses being sung inside by children who were forced
to go, incorporating a few rude gestures into their actions:

> Running over, running over,
> My cup's full and running over,
> Since the Lord's saved me,
> I'm as happy as can be;
> My cup's full and running over.

Then, with one final jeer they would run off, laughing and
free.

As I walk on, the rooks in the chestnut trees near the
church take over and I look across a field to where there
were once other fields where it was always summer, or so
it seems. Fields to which children could walk alone in
safety down grassy lanes and play all day with their
friends in meadows, unattended and without fear of
coming to any harm, other than getting a grazed knee
from falling over, or a bump on the head from a worn-out
cricket ball. Those were the days when childhood was
allowed its own company, its own space and freedom in
which to grow up, where the imagination could develop
without being overheard by adults. Not any more. Now it
is necessary for playtime to be supervised as well, even in
the countryside, and no one can believe in innocence
again.

The memory of one of those fields came home to me
recently in the strangest of ways and in the most unlikely
of places – southern Spain. My wife and I were staying
with a friend whose newly built house was very close to a
stretch of barren wasteland, which was undoubtedly
waiting for the developers to move in. I occasionally
walked across this stony ground to remind myself of what
human-beings can do to a land, creating ugliness out of
beauty, destroying a long history in their eagerness to
make a quick profit. I agree that it is sometimes true that
the natives themselves will have done nothing to preserve
their history or landscape from the speculators, but I was
saddened to see a country being disembowelled and so
wanted to absorb its wildness whilst it was still there. I
was certain that were I to return a year or two later it
would have disappeared altogether under another

urbanised heap of pseudo-Moorish villas, that the dusty
air would be smelling more of sun-tan lotion than
wildflowers. It was not without precedent.

At that moment a young boy passed by, stripped to the
waist and lost in his own ambitious dreams of what he
was going to be tomorrow, or the day after. He was
carrying a roughly hewn piece of wood which looked like
something between a baseball bat and a cricket bat. At the
same moment I also noticed that his back was badly
sun-burnt, his young skin raw and blistered. And, in that
instant, my mind fled back to a summer's day of more
than fifty years ago when I was his age and had gone with
the boy who lived next door to play cricket in a field not
far from the end of our street. It was a favourite
meeting-place. The owner of the field used it only for
grazing a few cows. They knew us as well as he did. The
grass was long and lush and filled with shining

The banks were embroidered with yellow flags

buttercups. The hawthorn hedges round the field always seemed to be in blossom and we sometimes searched them for birds' nests. The bottom of the field went down to a river where other boys regularly went to swim or to fish. The banks were embroidered with bright yellow flags and slowly darkening bulrushes.

On that particular day the sun shone as brassily as a large cymbal, vibrating with audible heat in a cloud-free sky. We took off our shirts, set up our stumps (at one end only) and measured out the pitch – twenty-two yards long. The thought of it now reminds me of how we learnt by heart our measure-tables at school – 'twelve inches one foot; three feet one yard; twenty-two yards one chain; ten chains one furlong ...' It's all history now, of course, like farthings, sixpences, florins and half-crowns. I can't remember whether we had a coin to toss that day to see who should bat first, but I lost and was forced to bowl. Francis, who was at March Grammar School, where they had sport, could bat well and he had probably never batted better in all his life than he did that day. As he scored, I scorched, until my back was as lobster-red as the boy's who passed me that morning on my walk.

Coincidence often breeds coincidence and, as I watched that boy swinging his makeshift bat through the Spanish air, a skylark rose from a nearby clump of grass, just as one had done that other day when eventually it was my turn to bat. Naturally, it completely ruined my concentration, otherwise this would have been a different story.

Those suddenly released memories were made even more poignant because I had heard only a few months earlier that Francis Redhead had died of a heart attack at the age of sixty, still working in the Yorkshire parish of Rothwell where he had been a priest for the past twenty-five years. We had hardly seen each other since those boyhood days but there, on that strange morning in a most unlikely place, he came back tall and athletic, smiling and fit, as if he was about to make another huge score at my expense. Then the image faded and I sat down on a rock to write these lines before the impact of memory was also lost:

> I did not think to write an elegy for you –
> A friend whom I'd not seen for forty years,

Until a boy passed by with sun-burnt skin,
And from the sky a lark spilt notes of rain.

Then I remembered one hot summer day
When we played cricket in long meadow grass,
Where cows stood watching every eager run
You notched in chalk upon your mellow blade.

I bowled for hours, shirt off, and unaware
Of how the heat was blistering my back,
Whilst you hit out, reluctant to declare
Until you'd equalled Bradman's highest knock.

Then, when my innings came, I had the luck
To be distracted by a lark that rose
As your late-swinger hit my middle stump.
I claimed 'no ball' but you'd hear none of that.

The hurt was worse than any peeling skin
And lasted for a month, or maybe more.
And so we parted company, still friends,
But never to recall our epic match.

Now houses crouch like fielders in the slips,
The grass is gone and there's no room to bat;
And you, I hear, at sixty have been caught
Whilst I, amazingly, am still not out.

That place, those hours, the summer I thought
lost,
Were all brought back because a boy passed by
Stripped to the waist and, from a heap of stones,
A new bird rose to haunt an empty sky.

Having had those particular memories re-awakened I
went later to see Francis's mother who still lives in
Whittlesey and is now in her eighty-eighth year. What
would she remember most of those days of sixty years ago
when we were neighbours? Mrs Redhead had lived in
Church Street since she was fourteen years old and did
not leave it until 1956, when our row of houses was pulled
down. I was to find that her affection for the place was
even deeper than mine:

I don't think there was another street like it anywhere.
They were such happy years. We had everything in a way,
didn't we! I know most of us were not very well off but

there's something more to life than that. As well as all those people you've mentioned, there were the Cleggs, Wilsons, Popelys, Carters, Mr White the solicitor and Mr Boyce the magistrate. In those days you could go out for a walk, or do some shopping, and you'd never have to worry about locking your door. Although we had some rum characters in the street we knew we could trust them because they were neighbours ... One of my happiest memories is of hearing the children in the Sunday Schools singing, especially at the Methodists. They had a big Sunday School then and I can still hear Mr Smith, the Superintendent shouting out 'if you don't shut up and be quiet you'll all be sent 'um!' And then there was the Salvation Army which had a good band in them days ...

Mrs Redhead's father was Mr Tom Blake who had the fish-and-chip shop and I had forgotten that at the bottom of his long garden there was a slaughter-house where one of the butchers in our street had his pigs killed:

I can remember the men filling the wooden tubs with boiling water before putting the pigs in and cutting their throats. It was a terrible noise, all that squealing and shouting, but it was the way things were done then. My dad used to help out where he could. When he collected his fish from the railway station early in the morning he would also pick up the daily papers to take to the shops. The fish came in big wooden crates and had to be scrubbed, gutted and cut up back at the house. That was one of my jobs before going off to school. I was often at work by 5 a.m., standing on bare, wet stone floors ... But enough of me, you have come to talk about Francis and I can see the pair of you now, making up games or talking seriously about all kinds of things. Because you were both fond of music you used to sing a lot, even when you played cowboys ...

The scenes came back to me with the freshness of the days themselves and I smiled to be reminded of those two lads in their long back garden, sitting beside a covered wagon made out of clothes-props and old blankets, singing 'Roll along prairie moon, roll along while I croon ...' to the accompaniment of a home-made guitar and a mouth-organ – the Tom Mix and Roy Rogers of Church Street. The as-yet-to-be priest and the unaware poet who had no idea how their lives would develop.

The friendship itself was not to develop much further for Francis went to the Grammar School in March and then to Cambridge University where he read English. At both places he excelled in athletics – hurdling, football and cricket, winning trophy after trophy. No wonder he beat me so convincingly in our epic one-a-side match. Having considered for a while that he would probably study law he eventually felt called to the priesthood and read theology. His love of sport, music and drama played an active part in his ministry, which was always sustained by a positive and practical spirituality. Today his parishioners recall with much affection his inspiring, eloquent sermons, and his patience. A gifted man indeed. I only wish the years and our circumstances had not separated us as much as they did. I just have to be grateful that another boy, in another land, reminded me of that place, those hours, and that summer I thought was forever lost.

If the street itself has a ghost, perhaps it is satisfied to know that we did not let it down.

Part 2

Fine Churches and a Few Encounters

Ah, but a man's reach should exceed his grasp.
Or what is heaven for?

Robert Browning

12   'Here of a Sunday Morning'

During the writing of this book more than a few people have asked me to explain what I meant by 'Fen Country Heaven'. Was I anticipating an early departure, or speaking of some world beyond our knowledge? Or was I simply, or rashly, suggesting that the Fens were really heaven on earth?

Although the last possibility is nearest to my intention it is still not the whole answer. So I will use this chapter to see if I can give a more satisfactory one.

To begin with, we have to find an acceptable definition of the word 'heaven'. Having consulted three main dictionaries I found that it could mean any of the following:

- the vault of sky overhanging earth;
- the upper regions of the air;
- a very great and indefinite height;
- one of the concentric revolving spheres imagined by the ancient astronomers;
- a dwelling-place for the gods and the blessed;
- a state of supreme happiness, or bliss;
  and, in the Christian sense of the word it denotes:
- the abode of the Deity – 'Our Father, which art in Heaven'.

But the Bible also – and often – uses it to describe the firmament, the place for the sun, moon and stars – 'Let there be lights in the firmament of the heavens' and so on.

So, is there more than one heaven, or only many names for the same indescribable regions of rapture and ecstasy, such as 'paradise', 'Nirvana', 'Utopia', 'the Elysian Fields'? A name that appeals to me is 'Fiddler's Green' – that happy land imagined by sailors where there is perpetual mirth, with a fiddle that never stops playing for dancers who never tire, and where there is always plenty of grog when the storms of life are over.

And how often we say, when speaking of someone who is blissfully happy, that he or she was 'in seventh heaven' – which is the ultimate state of joy and perfection.

It was certainly a word favoured by Shakespeare who much preferred 'heaven' to the word sky. Many other writers have used it to describe various levels of contentment or fulfilment. William Wordsworth, when writing of the French Revolution said, 'Bliss was it in that dawn to be alive/But to be young was very heaven.' Speaking of our earliest years he also said, 'Heaven lies about us in our infancy.' For the artist and designer William Morris it meant something else – 'Fellowship is heaven, and lack of fellowship is hell.' Sir Walter Scott went even further and wrote, 'For love is heaven, and heaven is love.' One of the most unusual definitions comes from a clergyman, the Reverend Sydney Smith, who said, 'My idea of heaven is eating *pâté de foie gras* to the sound of trumpets.' His preference would not meet with much approval these days.

I have already quoted Robert and Elizabeth Barrett Browning in the epigraphs to Part 1 and Part 2 of this book so have probably said enough to prove the flexibility of a word like 'heaven'. I will only repeat Mrs Browning's claim that 'Earth's crammed with heaven' and make sure that the Fen country is included in that belief.

Many readers will also recognize that the title of this chapter comes from the second verse of A.E. Housman's poem *Bredon Hill*:

> Here of a Sunday morning
> My love and I would lie,
> And see the coloured counties
> And hear the larks so high
> About us in the sky.

The poems in *A Shropshire Lad* were about a very different landscape and conveyed a spirit of sadness rather than joy. Housman was writing about 'the land of lost content' and the sorrows of war. But there was something in that particular line which appealed to me and set me thinking about the theme for the present pages.

Another influence that also helped to direct my thoughts came from Charles Dickens. I had just been re-reading a volume of his non-fiction, which can be just as entertaining as his novels. The essay that started me off was *City of London Churches*, in which he said:

> It came into my head one day, here I had been cultivating a familiarity with all the churches of Rome, and I knew nothing of the insides of the old churches of London! This befell on a Sunday morning. I began my expeditions that very same day, and they lasted me a year ...

Any idea that we might have that in Victorian times the churches were all packed to the doors, is soon dispelled by what Dickens tells us:

> As I stand at a street corner, I don't see as many as four people at once going to church, though I see as many as four churches with their steeples clamouring for people ...

He did slightly better the following week, choosing a smaller church 'of about the date of Queen Anne':

> As a congregation, we are fourteen strong; not counting the exhausted Charity School in a gallery, which has dwindled away to four boys and two girls ... The service books are musty, and the pulpit cushions are threadbare, and the whole of the church furniture is in a very advanced stage of exhaustion. We are three old women (habitual); two young lovers (accidental); two tradesmen, one with a wife and one alone; an aunt and nephew; again two girls (dressed out for church with everything about them limp that should be stiff, and *vice versa*): and three sniggering boys ...

One could accept that such a description might well fit a village church today, but a city church of more than a hundred years ago! Hard to believe, but it is true and, I can add that many of our country churches now present a very different picture.

With all these influences coming together I decided that I too would use a few Sunday mornings visiting some of the churches in the Fens, especially those that I already liked, mainly because I knew that they would at least be open on the Sabbath Day. I am aware that one can always apply for a key on weekdays when the churches will be locked but that is not always convenient and there is a lot of difference between a cold, empty building and an active one.

My first excursion was to Leverington, a village tucked in that quiet corner of Cambridgeshire, close to the borders of Lincolnshire and Norfolk, just north of Wisbech. Its fine, elegant spire can be seen from miles away, as slender as a stiletto. From the road from Fitten End to Gorefield it stands out like a needle-gauge on the horizon. It must have appeared as such to Oliver Goldsmith when he stayed with the Lumpkin family at Park Farm in 1771, when he was writing his play *She Stoops to Conquer*. There is a memorial tablet in the church to Anthony Lumpkin and one must assume that Goldsmith must have occasionally worshipped there with his hosts.

The church is dedicated to St Leonard, the patron saint of prisoners. The building has a mixture of styles and materials – bricks, stones, plain and decorated. The spire (now desperately in need of money to preserve it) sits in a nest of small turrets of the Norman tower. The clock is bold, plain and effective. The ornate south porch is fourteenth century, the high nave and clerestory fifteenth century, as is the beautiful Jesse window, though much restored. No one, I feel, would argue that Leverington parish church is one of the gems of the Fens. It also has some splendid gravestones in the churchyard, including one dated 1718 which tells us that 'A Modest Dutifull Child Lyeth Here Who was Beloved of her Father Dear – he at her Death did weep & moan ...' and was later to join her in the same plot. On the morning of my visit there was a congregation of some sixty or more worshippers who sang with an enthusiasm that some town churches could envy. After the service they welcomed me with a warm, eager friendliness and the offer of a cup of coffee. Without pretensions or reserve they spoke of their love for the place and the need to save the spire. Then they went about their usual after-service business of raising a little more money. Cooking-apples, jars of chutney and bazaar-tickets changing hands with the same keenness as the coffee and biscuits. I think Charles Dickens would have been impressed.

Gulls surveying the ploughed fields

By 11 a.m. the busy vicar was already anxious to get off to his next service which was to be at Wisbech St Mary's church. I was tempted to follow but the morning was too bright to give up, so I drove over to Gorefield and across the fen to Parson Drove and Throckenholt – a wonderful spot to see the extent of the Fens of both Lincolnshire and Cambridgeshire. The visibility across the land was outstanding, my view to the south uninterrupted for more than twelve miles over those fields I had been on earlier in the year with Alwyn Johnson. On the newly ploughed land scores of lapwings skipped about, leaping over each other as if they were playing draughts. From a nearby dyke a cautious heron lifted its grey body to a safer distance and in the sky a slow pageantry of subtle-coloured clouds completed the scene. 'Here of a Sunday morning' continued to ring through my head.

As I was in no hurry I ambled off to Gedney Hill, Holbeach Drove, Shepeau Stow and Crowland, where the

abbey looked splendid in the morning sun. I had forgotten
what a good view one gets of it from the Dowsdale side; it is
almost complete. Anyone familiar with previous volumes
will know that it is one of my favourite places in the Fens
and I could not resist another visit. Usually this is one spot I
like to have all to myself and I have spent hours alone in
those evocative ruins open to the sky. But a church is a
place of worship, not a museum, so it was good to see a
cheerful congregation emerging from its Sunday morning
service. History may have its highlights, its great events
and important people, but it is also a chronicle of customs
and continuity, and of the daily affairs of ordinary men and
women who are perpetuating what was, and always will
be.

The one thing that can be said about Fenland churches is
that they provide us with a considerable variety of interest
because they are so different. Towers, spires, roofs, por-
ches, belfries and chancels, shapes, sizes and building
materials all helping to represent the local characteristics.
Those with spires stand out especially in a landscape where
there are few heights or verticals. If Leverington has a fine
spire, what can be said of the one of Whittlesey St Mary's,
which many experts rightly consider to be the best in the
county! I used to pass it every day on my way to school and
never once missed looking up to the splendid weathercock
that shone on its crocketted pinnacle. It too can be seen
from miles away and, like Leverington's, needs a few
thousand pounds spending on it to keep it standing. How
impoverished and naked our landscape would be without
them. Even those churches without spires often have
sturdy, majestic towers that need the same degree of
maintenance – West Walton, Wisbech, Elm and Tydd St
Giles. All speak of our history and stand as a symbol of
human aspirations, constancy and traditions, whether they
are used for regular worship or simply as the right place in
which to be married, baptized, or buried. The prosperous
may still smell of furniture polish and incense, and have
fresh flower arrangements; the more neglected ones now
reek of damp, musty hymn books and Calor-gas fires, and
have flower arrangements which Dickens would call
'exhausted'. But they have all been important in the lives of
our communities and sometimes tell us more than we can
read in books.

One feature of our churches which, sadly, is disappearing rapidly is the churchyard with its ornate headstones over once respected graves. Names and tributes are now mostly obliterated, hidden either under a growth of lichen or erased by weather and time. Many, admittedly, displayed sentimental verse we could not live with now, but their individuality was often appealing, offering words of warning as much as comfort. There is one at Crowland, dated 1706, which reads:

> Man's life is like untoe [*sic*] a winter's daye.
> Some brake their faste and so depart awaye.
> Others stay dinner – then depart full fed.
> The longest age but supps and goes to bed.
> O reader, then behold and see,
> As we are now, so must ye be.

There is another, dated 1873, which I found particularly touching, recording the advice of a 41-year-old mother to her surviving family:

> Finally, children, Farewell.
> Be perfect, Be of good comfort.
> Be of one mind, Live in Peace,
> And the God of Love and Peace
>   Shall be with you.

It was my intention to write of only one more church visit before getting back to more general affairs because, unlike Charles Dickens, I do not have fifty-two Sunday mornings in which to make that many expeditions into every parish in the Fens worthy of mention. But so rich are we in exceptionally fine churches that I must carry this subject forward into the next chapter rather than skimp on a few passing references in this. Nor could I restrict myself to one only for there are too many deserving of anyone's attention. But which to choose? Should I revisit Boston, to comment again on its famous 'Stump' – which is anything but as its tower soars 272 feet into the sky; or should I go to St Mary's at Swineshead, or the rather quaint octagonal brick-built church at Moulton Chapel? With so many options I knew that I would have to trust to instinct, or perhaps even divine guidance. My own inclination was to go in the direction of the South Lincolnshire Marshlands and aim for somewhere like Gedney which, for many people in Lincolnshire, is considered the 'cathedral of the Fens'.

My instinct and divine guidance were in total agreement and our decision proved to be rewarding and successful. How often we find that luck breeds luck, that some days just can't help being perfect. I would have been content with one prize but there were bonuses.

13   The Unearthliness of Things

The morning sky was the colour of apricots, the wet misty earth a damson blue. It was a wonderful day to go exploring and I began my expedition from where I had left off, at Crowland. From there I made my way to Holbeach Drove, Holbeach St Johns and Fleet, exhilarated by the light, freedom and solitude. The land was well-groomed, as if waiting for some great ceremony with the mellowing year. Newly ridged furrows showed where the next crops of potatoes would be. Wheat was already established in its combed pattern across the fields. There was a sense of purpose and well-established order.

I felt myself drawn willingly towards the buried shores of the Wash, where those Lincolnshire churches of Holbeach, Fleet, Gedney and Long Sutton lined the then existing coastline like fortresses before man pushed the waters further out to sea.

My first stop was at Fleet where one of the best approaches to the church is through the uncommon thatched lych-gate and churchyard. I was immediately impressed by the number of old gravestones that were still standing in their orderly rows. So many generations, so large a population? Why? Where had they all come from?

Visitors are frequently puzzled by the grandeur of some of our churches in areas where there appears to be no more than a handful of houses. But, as was pointed out to me, a church was not just representative of the village around it but of the parish, and some fenland parishes are scattered over a large area. We also have to remember that the medieval population of the Fens was relatively larger than it is today, that churches were built, not only to the glory of God but as symbols of prosperity. If the church was to be the gateway to immortality then it was best not to be too stingy with the investments or donations. Piety was frequently a mask behind which lurked more earthly ambitions.

But I have to say that I was instantly won over at Fleet by the church which is dedicated to St Mary Magdalene. Another unusual feature is the tower and spire which are detached from the main building. It looked as if, in the end, the builders lacked the confidence to put one on top of the other. Had they done so the church would have been a close rival to the neighbouring one at Gedney. As it turned out they were wise to separate the tower from the nave because the spire (like so many others in the Fens) recently needed a few thousand pounds spending on it to make it safe.

I was lucky at Fleet because on the morning that I arrived two men were about to unload some trestle-tables for a forthcoming bazaar, so the church was opened for me. Immediately I felt there was something special about the interior. It had a lovely atmosphere and was clearly cared for by its parishioners. The two men were obviously proud of it and regularly interrupted their labours to point out to me some of the church's most interesting features – the gargoyles, windows and especially the list of rectors who had served there since the early thirteenth century. There was one entry – or rather three – which spoke quietly of a period of history when, for a few years, this country was not ruled by the monarchy. The Reverend Robert Haselwood was the incumbent from 1627–43; then Oliver Cromwell disposed of him and put in one of his own men – Samuel Panke, to supervise the worship; then, with the restoration of the monarchy, the Reverend Robert Haselwood was re-installed in 1660 and served until 1684.

But the name that attracted me most was that of the Reverend James Ashley because I had just read on the north wall of the chancel one of the most eloquent memorial inscriptions I had seen anywhere:

Beneath is interr'd all that was mortal
of the REVEREND JAMES ASHLEY
Twenty-two years Rector of this Parish
A Man whose admirable and highly cultivated powers of
mind were only equalled by the generosity and goodness
of his heart, Who after a life spent in conscientious

Discharge of the Sacred Duties of his Profession,
Tho' worn down with continual affliction
which He bore with Christian Fortitude,
Calmly resigned his Soul into the Hands of his Maker –
on August 7th 1806 – Aged 63 years.

Having been urged by the two gentlemen of Fleet not to miss Gedney, I continued my pilgrimage into that mysterious and haunting kingdom of the Lincolnshire Marshlands where life exists even today in an uncertain truce between the land and the sea, between reality and unreality.

If I have praised other fenland churches to the best of my ability then I truly found myself searching for words to describe this great church, also dedicated to St Mary Magdalene, for it is undoubtedly worth travelling miles to see. Words like 'breathtaking', 'magnificent' and 'beautiful' are just not adequate. They have been used too often to describe less worthy buildings. It is so ethereal it has the appearance of not having been built by mortal hands. It looks as if it was created somewhere in space and settled here in the Fens. It is so spacious and light that it seems, as one writer so aptly said, 'to be almost transparent', as if sculpted out of a cloud with windows.

The long paved path to the south porch gives one time to prepare for each delight. The exterior needs time. It is difficult to believe that so much stone could appear so weightless, so gossamer-like. Slowly the eye rises to take in the long clerestory with its twelve clear windows, then moves to the imposing tower with its small pyramidal spire perched on top like a candle-snuffer. Even then one is not physically aware of the building's substance. This only comes with touching the mighty entrance door of mediaeval wood. It exudes history.

Dare I say that, for a few moments, the interior is slightly disappointing? It is impressively wide and well-kept, but much of it is modern, with rows of stacking chairs that look out of place. Better to look upwards again to the fine timber roof and then to walk slowly towards the chancel.

It was there where I read another memorial tablet that intrigued me. This was to:

RICHARD LAWSON GALES
Vicar of this Parish – 1909–1927
Priest, Poet and Essayist,
Who entered into rest 26th December, 1927
in his 65th year.
This tablet was erected by his
Parishioners and Friends.

The high altar is reached by three steps which divide the carved and solid stone altar rail. Again I was torn between this fluctuating impression of the substantial and the insubstantial. One moment the fleeting air of the place made one feel it could simply disappear like a mirage. The next moment there was something which spoke of its everlastingness. So what was real, and what was unreal? When I stepped up to the lectern to see what the last lesson read from the Bible had been, my uncertainties were further compounded. The book was open at St Mark, chapter 13, verse 1:

> And as he went out of the temple, one of his disciples saith unto him, 'Master, see what manner of stones and what buildings are here!' And Jesus answering said unto him, 'Seest thou these great buildings? There shall not be left one stone upon another, that shall not be thrown down.'

As I drove away I was almost afraid to look back, fearing that the building might have already disappeared, that it had been no more than a figment of my imagination, a ghost ship that had sailed in from the past to be stranded at low tide on the edge of civilization. But it was still there, dimly outlined like a fine engraving on the clear glass of the sky.

What had made my journey that day so refreshingly unfrustrating was the almost total absence of traffic on the roads. Although I always choose to take 'the road less travelled by' I am not fortunate enough to have the route to myself every time. But, if good fortune had been with me since leaving home, it continued to stay with me as I drove back. For miles I did not pass, nor was I passed by, another vehicle. From Gedney Broadgate, along Delph Bank to Holbeach St Johns, Holbeach Drove and Dowsdale, was like driving over a private, sparsely populated kingdom in which any period of history would not have looked out of place. The glories of the morning had at last given way to a cold east wind. The glow had gone from the earth which now looked unpoetically wet, bloodless and dead, a black mass discarded by the sea, waiting for some kind of resurrection. It would come. The desert would blossom again. The change in the weather did not dampen my spirits. I was on a high. The choice I had made, if indeed I had made it, could not have been bettered. The scribbled notes in my pocket, the scenes still vivid in my mind, were all eager to find some permanence on the page.

I doubt now if the words that survived do justice to the day. They seldom do. There are some feelings that language cannot express, nor can music, or art. Even if all three came together in some heavenly composition of peace and joy, they could still not give wings to the overwhelming sense of gratitude for such a day.

14   At the Heart of the Matter

Slowly, and not for long enough, the brash monotony of summer's colours gave way to the more subtle shades of autumn. After all those weeks and miles of harvest-yellow the land began to regain a pattern that entertained the eye with constant variety. Great squares of green, brown and black chequered the Fens beneath a mellowing sun.

I was on one of my favourite journeys again, travelling by train to Ely. On either side of the track were vistas that seldom fail to delight at that time of the year – ploughed fields, as yet unharrowed, so that the furrows of chunky soil shone with sunlight; acres that had already been harrowed, making the crumbled earth appear brushed and docile; crops of unharvested sugar-beet whose leaves were limpish yellow in their first stages of decay; and then the emerald green shoots of winter-wheat like fine stitches on a garment still in the making. Each field was bordered by the paler green of grass on the sides of the dykes, below which the narrow veins of water shone as silver as mercury in a barometer.

Nor were these just picturesque scenes to please the idle traveller. Even though it was a Saturday and already mid-afternoon, men were busy working on the land, ploughing, harrowing, drilling. Behind them the usual flurry of gulls, swirling and tumbling like white leaves tossed up by the wind. And, above the land, an even vaster acreage of sky resembling an uncharted ocean on which sat islands of clouds waiting to be conquered and named – unknown countries slowly drifting in from the silent chaos of creation. As they passed beneath the sun they cast huge shadows on the land, projecting their anonymity on to the familiar features already there. Where the shadows fell the colours were intensified, in the way that the sea is when clouds pass.

Lowering my eyes from the sky to those more acceptable limits of earth I was struck by the sudden smallness of things. Farmhouses and red-roofed barns now seemed no more than toy buildings. Rows of tilting telegraph-poles were as stalks of straw left uncut by the harvesters. It took time to adjust. Such magnificent space. Such beauty. I wondered if the train-driver, sitting up there alone in his cab, was seeing it all with the same eye, the same sense of joy and appreciation. How ever many journeys he made, no two trips could ever be alike. Perhaps he was too occupied with his job, with looking at signals or watching for obstacles on the line. If he was, I trust I was suitably grateful, but I still thought it must be a satisfying way of earning a living on such a day.

Slowly the train began the gradual rise towards Ely and I could feel the extra pull as we approached the island. Strangers are often surprised to hear us talk of 'islands' but they are still one of the natural features of the black Fens. The keen eye can always trace their positions, shapes and boundaries. Most of the towns and villages in the Cambridgeshire Fens were, of course, built on islands – Ramsey, Whittlesey, Thorney, March, Chatteris, Manea and Ely, which is the largest of them all. Although now deprived of the surrounding water that originally made them islands, it is still obvious that these old communities were built on the clay or gravel elevations that were not inundated by the great flood which created the Fens. The island of Ely was roughly ten miles across at its widest point and rose appreciably above the submerged land, providing an admirable dais for the city's magnificent cathedral.

I walked from the station and through the parklands to the south side of that great building. What an architectural wonder it is. It impresses from every aspect but the view from the south is enhanced by the trees in the foreground as one's eyes are inevitably led up to the tower. I suppose the greatest miracle of all is that it is still there for, over its long history, it has been threatened many times, by man as much as by nature.

Its ecclesiastical beginnings go back to the seventh century when Etheldreda founded the first abbey, for monks as well as nuns. She must have been a very remarkable lady who, already widowed, became the wife of the king of Northumbria with whom, as the Venerable Bede wrote, 'she lived twelve years and yet remained always a pure and glorious virgin'.

Etheldreda had desired a religious life from when she was a girl and eventually managed to persuade her husband to release her so that she could follow her vocation. In 673 she moved into East Anglia to establish the church of which she was to become abbess. By her humility, charity and example, she became known as 'the Virgin Mother of many virgins, dedicated to God'.

One of the legends concerning her is that on her arrival one night in the Fens she rested by the wayside and thrust her walking-staff into the ground. When she woke in the morning she found that it had taken root and was bearing both leaves and fruit. This was a sign she had been waiting for and Ely was to be the place where her ministry was to begin.

Sadly she was to remain in office as the first abbess for only six years because she died on 23 June 679 and was buried in a plain wooden coffin in the churchyard. Her sister, Sexburga, who succeeded her, eventually had the body re-buried in the church on 17 October 695. Soon reports of miraculous healings at Etheldreda's shrine began to circulate through the Fens, and beyond. It was told that when her body was exhumed it was still free from corruption and mortal decay, even though it had been buried in the earth for sixteen years. It was not an uncommon claim during those times. Forty years later the same reports were being made about St Guthlac of Crowland Abbey. Of such stuff are legends made. So it was not long before Ely became an essential place of pilgrimage, bringing believers, followers, curiosity-mongers and cynics from all over England. If Etheldreda had managed to attract a great deal of wealth to her abbey when alive, she continued to do so most effectively in death.

The abbey was to remain untroubled and admired for nearly 200 years until the Danes came to exercise their swords on yet another defenceless religious community. Although recent studies of the Norsemen's incursions into this country have tried to show that they were not entirely indiscriminate escapades of pillage, rape and theft, they

Interior of the Lantern Tower, Ely Cathedral

still appear to have had little respect for places of worship which they saw as the strongholds of riches as well as religion. But at Ely they at least found a breed of men who were prepared to fight to the death to protect their abbey and lands. The battle for Ely was to be one of the bloodiest and most costly campaigns the Vikings encountered on English soil. The abbey was burnt to the ground and it looked as if Etheldreda's vision of a house of prayer that would last for a thousand years had come to an end. Far from it. By 970 a new Benedictine abbey was being consecrated, albeit for monks only this time, but the religious life of the island was resumed. By 1081 the abbot was able to announce plans for an exciting new building programme to enlarge the church and give it the best tower in Europe. We shall never know whether that dream was fully realized because the tower collapsed in 1322, leaving the sanctuary and transepts open to the sky.

The need to rebuild was immediate and positive. Out of the rubble was to rise what is undoubtedly one of the most inspiring structures to be seen anywhere – the octagon tower and lantern. The task for designing and building the tower was entrusted to the sacrist, Alan Walsingham and the carpenter, William Hurley, who was also carpenter to Edward III. What they achieved was itself another miracle for their tower was to span seventy-four feet and support the lantern's eight massive pillars of oak sixty-three feet high. This amazing construction of timber and lead weighed 400 tons and was to dominate the Cambridgeshire landscape for the next 600 years. It still does, even though it has been attacked by the death-watch beetle and has survived modern wars as well as floods and pollution. Its concept would have been staggering in any age. To know that it was built in the fourteenth century leaves one speechless in admiration. I have seen it when it appears to rise ethereally out of the mist and when it sits as solid as a mountain in a wilderness. I have seen it silhouetted against the early morning sun and floodlit at night under the winter stars. It is as if it can change its mood with the time of day or season of the year.

But Ely is not just an impressive cathedral. The city's history is alive with all kinds of dramas, riots, political unrest, educational excellence and artistic achievement. One of its famous residents was Oliver Cromwell, whose troops wantonly defaced the glorious Lady Chapel. People in the Fens still have mixed feelings about the man who reigned as Lord Protector of England from 1653 to 1658. Born in Huntingdon in 1599, Cromwell was a local farmer and landowner before going into politics, convincing the fenmen that if they would support him, he would always support them – a promise which he forgot when he gained the most powerful position in the land. He was not the first, nor the last, to wriggle out of such a commitment when it suited him. His part in the Civil War, from 1642 to 1649, gave him an awesome reputation. But, to a fenman, honour is worth more than victory in the field, or authority in parliament. When the time came the fenlanders were to find themselves without a leader in their own struggles to protect their lands. Many felt that Cromwell had betrayed them.

Nevertheless, one cannot visit Ely without sparing some time to look at the house where he lived from 1636 to 1646. It was already an old house when he moved in, with parts

Oliver Cromwell's House, Ely

of it dating back to the fourteenth century. I like to think that William Hurley stayed there whilst the new tower was being erected. Now part of it is used as the city's tourist information centre – and very good it is too.

One of Ely's more loveable and creative residents today is the well-known writer and novelist, Sybil Marshall, who can entertain for hours with her memories of life in the Fens of more than eighty years ago. Not only can she capture the humour and philosophy of Fen people but also their accent, and at last we have someone who is preserving in literature a detailed picture of that race of independent families who created their own legends during the first half of this century. Through her others can now enter what was once an almost secret world and her readers extend far beyond our native shores.

Whatever Ely's claims are, it remains firmly at the heart of the matter when talking about the Fens and, so far, it has not been utterly ruined by modernization and commercial take-overs, though there are some signs of it creeping in.

On that early autumn Saturday afternoon the little city gave me the impression of a village bursting at the seams. When I emerged from the serene spaciousness of the cathedral and walked into the High Street, I was taken by surprise to find so many people thronging the pavements, window-gazing, chatting, strolling along and perhaps already beginning to fret over what to buy all their relatives for Christmas. I entertained the hope that some of them would be making their way down Forehill to Bennett's Bookshop where I was due to do a signing-session of my then latest book – *Fen Country Christmas*. A few did, it is true, but regrettably Forehill is one street in Ely that does appear to get ignored by shoppers these days. It is as if life ends at the Market Place – and it doesn't. Admittedly, my two hours there were pleasant enough and I had some interesting conversations with my customers. As one of my fenland friends would say, you can only really talk to one person at a time if you're to pay any attention. And that is one thing that fenmen do expect.

My journey home was just as beautiful as my journey there. Between sundown and moonrise the water in the dykes had the stillness of stainless steel reflecting the opaque light of the sky. The coloured patterns of the fields were less obvious and my gaze then more hypnotically fixed on the setting sun. Close by, a long black cloud lay grounded like a monstrous oil-tanker on the horizon. Smaller clouds soon caught fire and the sky throbbed with red and gold. As I watched that spectacular sunset develop I heard a couple of passengers talking behind me.

'Not a lot to see out there, is there.'

'No,' said the other, 'I think it's a dreadful place. Give me mountains any day of the week.'

But, I wanted to say, you wouldn't get a sunset like that if there were great heaps of rock in the way. I kept quiet and let them go on talking about the places they thought were beautiful whilst I watched in awe as the dying sun slipped below the skyline. It had tried so hard.

As that moment came to an end an almost full moon rose from the eastern horizon, persuading the traveller that out there the world was not only flat instead of round but also motionless, a fixed and constant axle on which the rest of the universe revolved. Beyond that vast expanse of sky what other acts of creation were taking place? What other suns and moons were there? If autumn was bringing all shades of colour back into our world, so too was it restoring the interest of the night sky, with stars glowing more brightly in their appointed places. News of recently discovered galaxies and the birth of stars larger than the whole of our galaxy, did not intimidate. It increased the wonder. The familiar stars which I was able to observe were, after all, born in similar fashion millions of years ago, and they had not harmed us. It was exciting simply to be part of an even greater cosmic existence than the one we already acknowledged. Were there Fens on other planets too? Better sunsets? A sharper quality of light? Someone trying to make sense of it all? How much did we shine in their firmaments? What if the gates of space were suddenly to open and I could see the true marvels of creation? Why be frightened? Perhaps living in the Fens helps to prepare us for the unknown, if not the answers.

There are times, I'm sure, when my wife worries about me when I go on these trips by train to Ely, as if the journeys play too many tricks on my imagination. How else could I achieve such ecstasy? Certainly not from the drinks trolley which either doesn't exist or, as on that particular excursion of which I have just written, was 'malfunctioning' and unable to make its way down the aisle of the coach. No, the only spirit to raise my blood-pressure to those levels of satisfaction and delight, is the spirit of the Fens itself – neat, undiluted and marvellously potent.

15   Where the Streets
were Made for Talking

If, during my many years of writing about the Fens, I had
still managed to say very little about such places as
Christchurch, Wimblington and Isleham, some reader
might feel compelled to ask why I have never devoted a
chapter or two to the important town of March.

I am not sure that I can give a satisfactory answer to that
question either, but I think there may be a couple of
subconscious reasons. My earliest memory of March is of
the day when I – and a train-load of boys from Whittlesey
– were sent off one Saturday morning to sit our
eleven-plus examination to see if any of us were worthy of
a place at the Grammar School. Apparently very few of us
were and we could not wait to shake off the dust of the
town from our feet as we hurried back to the station, then
home and the anonymity of failure.

The other reason, I believe, is more professional in that I
did not want to trespass too much into another writer's
territory. Mr Trevor Bevis is a local historian who has
written many useful booklets about the Fens and the
history of March. In the same way that I have tried not to
plough the same furrows as Sybil Marshall, so have I
attempted not to encroach on Mr Bevis's patch, which he
has cultivated so well.

I feel now that I can come to terms with both reasons or,
if they have only been excuses, to take pen in hand and
offer my own impressions from the safety of my room.

Although other writers in the past have not always been
over-generous in their praise of the town, no one can deny
that it is a very interesting, challenging place, enjoying its
most prosperous days no doubt when its railway marshal-

ling yards were among the largest in Britain.

There was a time, however, when it was considered little more than a village near the larger town of Doddington, which was once the largest parish in the country. Even when Daniel and Samuel Lysons published their volume on Cambridgeshire (1809) as part of their vast history, *Magna Britannia*, March contained only '555 houses'.

It did not have to wait for the coming of the railways to improve on that small population because it was, after all, set in the middle of some very rich fenland and, once the agricultural depression of the early nineteenth century was over, farmers and market gardeners were to bring some prosperity to the town before a single rail track was laid. But the railways and light industries did make a difference – and that, perhaps, is why March had never had what I feel to be a true fenland identity in the way that Ely and Wisbech have. It is true that it has always been well-known for its independence, but how would one describe its real character? Was it different from any other country town, irrespective of its setting? Did it reflect the indigenous quality of the Fens? This is a contentious issue to bring into these premature impressions and they may change. For the moment I am the silent traveller, the observer, looking at the place as if for the first time.

The town, of course, was not so completely unknown to me for, even as a child, I had passed through it by train many times on my way to the Norfolk coast for the family's annual holidays at Hunstanton or Heacham. And, now I come to think of it, I spent a few weeks working there when I was a junior clerk for a firm of solicitors in Peterborough. They were planning to expand their practice and opened a small office in Wisbech and then in March. I was consigned to both places in turn, as a kind of daytime caretaker sitting in a bare room, waiting to answer the telephone or to attend to the first nervous client who climbed up the narrow stairs. I don't think I could have been very successful for I seem to recall that I spent most of my time staring out of the window – the habit which my former schoolteacher told me I had even when I was six years old. In both towns the office overlooked the river. At Wisbech it was the present-day River Nene which flows to its outfall at Guy's Head and into the Wash; and at March I had the old River Nene, reduced now almost to a trickle before making its way to join the Great Ouse and its outfall at King's Lynn. In both places I must have navigated many an imaginary trip down those waterways to freedom just to prevent myself fossilizing with boredom. Only one memory stands out from my brief sojourn in March and that is of a lady getting knocked down by a cyclist as she ran across the road to a fish-and-chip shop. The bicycle was, I'm sure, injured far worse than either of the two people involved, but it was a moment of drama in an otherwise benign day.

As those random memories made their way to the surface I began to understand even more why I had avoided March. But now I decided to delay no longer and so set off, without pride or prejudice, to find out what I would think about the place all those years later. March, like Ely, was once an island and I am persuaded to believe this is one of the reasons why true Fen people are so independent. They are really 'islanders' who were forced to be self-sufficient and made to govern their lives by their own rules, with little interference from outside. Drainage may have taken away the waters which once separated those communities for half the year, but the local attitudes and characteristics have not been so easily eradicated.

Having decided to visit March by road I nevertheless chose to avoid the obvious route which I knew would be busy, and set out from Yaxley, via Holme Fen, Ramsey St

A giant bog-oak pulled out by a plough

Mary's and Doddington. As most of the crops had now
been lifted and the fields re-ploughed, I witnessed again
one of the phenomena of the Fens – the massive black
bog-oaks that are annually ploughed up to remind us of an
age when the Fens were densely covered with forests. But
when the land was in a perpetual state of being flooded,
becoming as Daniel Defoe accurately described as 'the
sink of thirteen counties', the trees slowly died and fell
into the swampy waters. Beneath the water the peat was
already forming from their decayed foliage and it was this
wet bed that was to preserve them. Some of those
bog-oaks can be of great antiquity. I have some
napkin-rings that were hand-carved out of a piece of
bog-oak that was estimated to be 22,000 years old. The
ones in Holme Fen are probably no more than 5,000 years
old but when one is pulled out of its hiding place it can lie
on the side of the road for years, like some fossilized giant
or fertility god that went to sleep and never woke up.
Many were sixty feet tall and, in their buried state, can
ruin a ploughshare that has the misfortune to strike it in
the shrinking soil. One farmer told me that it was like a
ship hitting an iceberg. Having got them out of his land a
farmer can do little with them, other than burn them.
When wet the wood is difficult to saw through because it
is very fibrous and, if left too long to dry, then it becomes
impossible to cut because it sets as hard as iron. Smaller
trees are often left in heaps on the headlands to dry out or
rot until they can be burnt. Although they are commonly
called bog-oaks not all of them are. Many are yew, fir or
hazel. But all are a nuisance to the farmer. Some years ago
a bog-oak was found at Stretham, near Ely, which was
82-foot long and weighed eight tons.

Ugly though they are one cannot cease to be amazed by
them and all the history that was buried with them –
history that predates the beginning of Christianity and
Ancient Egypt. What beasts rummaged beneath those
branches? What birds nested in those boughs? Did early
man camp in their shade? If only they could speak.

It would have been easy to stay because there was a
stillness on the land that lured and I was tempted to drive
up to the buried shores of Whittlesea Mere and partake of
the silence there. But I could not put off my visit to March
any longer. Ramsey St Mary's, Ramsey Forty Foot and

Doddington had to be just a means to an end – well, almost. How can anyone rush through the Fens when the light is as cut-crystal sharp as it was that day. It was as if the already expansive landscape had been put under a magnifying glass. I had seldom seen such great distances. The eye could not take in the space or the light. Repeatedly I stopped in amazement to gasp in wordless wonder at the scenes around me. On one side of the road a newly ploughed field glistened, its huge chunks of soil shining like roughly-hewn Welsh coal, black and sparkling. On the other side the river-water flashed like a roll of silver foil. In the middle distance, tractors criss-crossed backward and forwards over a field like slow shuttles over a dark loom. In the far distance were the boundaries of Norfolk to the north-east and the old county of Huntingdonshire to the south-west. But so vast was the plain on which I stood that boundaries ceased to matter, or to exist. There was only one and that was infinity.

Am I never going to get to March, you ask? Yes, and it was a good day to be there. The moment I walked into Broad Street I bumped into John Cole, an old neighbour from my Church Street days in Whittlesey of more than fifty years ago. We stopped to catch-up on the gossip of half-a-century ago. Then he looked at his watch and said, 'I'm sorry, but I must dash. I've promised to meet a friend at Heathrow later this morning.' Heathrow, via March? Who dare accuse us of being provincial!

By the time I had been in the town for an hour I was aware that it was a place where people had time to stand and talk. So often these days shopping is a frantic rush, especially in cities where we are up against thousands of others shopping and also trying to beat the car-parking charges. But at March there were no such charges, so that was one pressure removed. As I walked up and down Broad Street and High Street I frequently had to step off the pavement because a group of people were engrossed in talking about everything under the sun – going to the doctor; refusing to take the medicine he'd prescribed; putting mother in a home; falling out with the vicar; how to get a rent rebate; the best thing for piles; the price of fish; and what they thought about Princess Diana. Serious stuff! It was as if the rest of the world could pass by and it wouldn't matter. Those pavement philosophers sounded

confident enough to govern the country. Now, there's a
thought.

The town of March – and the name means boundary –
had existed since Saxon times and probably goes back
even further. Recent excavations in the Fens have proved
we need to reconsider the beginnings of some of our
communities. Beneath the earliest known footprints were
often footprints before and, as has been shown at Flag
Fen, the moment one layer is removed another is revealed.

Next to Ely, March was the largest island in the Fens
before the great Bedford Level was created in the
seventeenth century. There are still fragments of those
former years. Tucked away in odd corners are some
charming and often quaint buildings whose haphazard
architecture is a welcome relief from so much modern
conformity. I know someone who judges a town by its
street-lamps. I find roofs and chimneys far more
interesting, and March has some old roofs that are most
attractive.

The course of the old River Nene tends to cut the town
in half but the riverside is not without its appeal and rural
charm. Some of the waterside houses and gardens are
more than 300 years old and counteract any suggestion
that the town centre makes of trying to quicken its image.
On the day that I was there several colourful narrow-boats
were moored close to the shops, adding to the feeling of
leisure.

The market itself was busy in a casual sort of way, with
stallholders calling out their wares and the smell of
hot-dogs and fried onions making me feel a little peckish.
A local radio-station interviewer was trying to gather some
opinions about something or other and, by the look of
desperation on his troubled face, wasn't having much luck
in arousing controversy. For a bit of fun I decided to see
what I could do, without a microphone.

The first lady I spoke to said, 'It's no good you asking
me. I'm from Doddington.' Well, quite. That is four miles
away.

I then stopped a man who was probably well into his
seventies. 'March seems to be pretty lively these days –
what do you think of it?' I asked.

'Too busy,' he said. 'Too many damn cars. Takes nigh
on a bloody hour to cross the road.'

I had to agree with him. Everywhere's the same. The Fens could be a paradise but for the volume of traffic that now pounds all day through our streets.

But March has many things to be proud of and one of them is the church of St Wendreda, famous for its fifteenth-century double-hammerbeam roof of 120 carved angels, which Sir John Betjeman said it would be worth cycling forty miles into a headwind to see. But I wonder how many casual visitors to the town actually see it, situated as it is on the south side of the main shopping centre and a tidy walk away? They could well miss seeing one of the finest interior roofs in England.

So, I had to concede that March was more than a once-upon-time railway town or the graveyard of so many fen boys' educational aspirations. It was more than just an ordinary town with no great sense of its past and little to contribute to the future. It had its place in the Fens and was a lively but relaxed, friendly but cautious community that seemed perfectly at ease with itself. As the brief guide to the town says, it is 'an ideal base for exploring the Fens and for participating in the specialist activities that the area has to offer'. These include boating, bird-watching, fishing, archaeology, cycling, music, golf, keep-fit and micro-flying. And the people of March still find time to talk when they're out shopping? Long may it be so.

I cannot leave the town without recounting the experience of another writer, Hilaire Belloc, who was not as fortunate in his efforts to visit the town and, in particular, the Griffin Inn. In his collection of essays, *The Hills and the Sea* (1906) he recalls how someone in London had advised him to try this Fenland hostelry, with which 'no inn could compare'. He was told that not many people had heard of March but everyone had heard of the Griffin. So he set out for the Fens and 'came at the very beginning of them to a great ditch, which barred all further progress'. He wandered up and down the bank for an hour, wondering how on earth he was going to get to the famous inn, when he met a fenman 'who was sadder and more silent than even the vast level and lonely land in which he lived'. He asked the man how one could cross the dyke. The man said he didn't know. Hilaire Belloc then asked if he had heard of the Griffin. Again he said no. 'And,' said the writer, 'still the great ditch stood between me and my pilgrimage', commenting also that 'these dykes of the Fens are accursed things'. Eventually, after many frustrated and abortive attempts to reach March, he found a man with a horse and cart who was going through the town and was prepared to give him a lift. For some reason that I cannot understand Hilaire Belloc found that 'the horses in the Fens are like no other horses in the world for speed', which was a disadvantage because the particular horse that was conveying him went so fast that the cart, driver and passenger had passed through March before the author had time to learn its name – 'It went so fast that before I knew what had happened the Griffin had flashed by me and was gone.' By the time he realized what had happened he was two miles on the other side of the town and could only 'affirm with faith that the inn is the noblest house of call in the Fens'.

I, clearly, had fared much better and had enjoyed both the town and the inn. So it was with gratitude that I drove back, slowly, over the Fens with their 'accursed dykes', reassured that they do not yield their inns or secrets easily to anyone from outside.

16   The Pattern of Encounters

Many years ago a friend of mine, Bill Turner, wrote a poem with the opening lines:

> It only takes one poet to spoil a sunset:
> At the first metaphor the sky pales in alarm ...

So when some more recent friends, who were visiting the Fens for the first time, asked where I would take them to view one of these renowned fenland exhibitions of heavenly splendour, I naturally hesitated. Sunsets do not need a commentary. They speak for themselves. They are for watching, preferably in silence. Why not just point my visitors in the right direction and let them get on with it?

It isn't as easy as that. Sunsets are not necessarily daily displays that can be taken for granted. We can go for weeks without seeing more than an exhausted ember on the horizon, when the ash-coloured sky is untouched by the sun's dying. Fenmen may be pretty good at conjuring up reasons for all sorts of things but they are not magicians who can pull sunsets out of the hat. As I have said elsewhere, miracles are unpredictable.

Yet, even if I were able to say when one of these pyrotechnic extravaganzas would take place, where in the Fens would I choose to take anyone to share in the excitement and wonder? There would have to be a river or a dyke close by for the best sunsets need water as well as sky. I am greedy for the reflection as well as the reality.

Fortunately there are many vantage points where long stretches of water mirror the heavens at any time of day or night. I have seen some spectacular sunsets from Ten Mile Bank looking across Hilgay Fen and the Welney Washes, and witnessed some memorable ones from Benwick looking over towards Ramsey, or from the more elevated

The best sunsets need water as well as sky

level of Deeping High Bank I have watched the setting sun
spread its glories over John Clare country fading darkly
into Northamptonshire.

The Helpston poet was superb at describing skies and
sunsets, even when they were not wildly dramatic:

> The sunshine's gone & now an April evening
> Commences with a dim & mackerel sky.
> Gold light & woolpacks in the west are leaving
> And leaden streaks their splendid place supply.
> Sheep ointment seems to daub the dead-hued sky
> And night shuts up the lightsomeness of day
> All dark & absent as a corpse's eye …

There is nothing over-romantic or too poetical about that.
Clare makes it sound very matter of fact and earthly. But

that was his strength.

Spring is arguably the best time for sunsets in the Fens. The lengthening days give the sky more time to play about with the jostling clouds and wealth of shades. They are more subtle than the fierce fires of autumn, less sudden than those of winter that will leave a snowy landscape blood-soaked for five minutes and then expire.

A man who often comes to mind when I am thinking of sunsets is someone with whom I worked some forty years ago. His name was Reg Oswin and he had recently retired from a career in the Civil Service, for which he had been awarded the Imperial Service Order. He had come to live in Crown property in the village of Holme, near Yaxley. Although he soon made himself busy in parish affairs he still had time to spare and was determined not to get bored living in the Fens. So he took a part-time job as a book-keeper with the Whittlesey firm of L.C. Giddens Ltd, where I also put in a few hours. He liked the village of Holme for it was close to the A1 should he ever feel the need to escape back to the south of England, to London or Reigate, where he had been very active in amateur productions of Gilbert and Sullivan. Not many days in the office passed without some excerpt being sung or whistled for us. Sometimes he made up his own words to go with familiar tunes, or used well-known notices for the same purpose, such as 'No Hawkers, No Circulars, Beware of the Dog'.

As well as his ISO he was equally proud of a fading photograph which he frequently produced from his wallet. It was of himself with two small girls, one on each hand, running across the lawn at a Civil Service garden party. The two girls, who he was rushing to the safety of a marquee to escape the sudden downpour of a July thunderstorm, were the then Princess Elizabeth and her sister Princess Margaret. A press-photographer had snapped them and the picture was published in one of the daily national newspapers. He could have had no idea how often that photograph would be shown, or how happy it had made one man.

Mr Oswin's mother had worked as a milliner's assistant to Queen Victoria. The shop was in Old Bond Street and the girls lived on the premises, working from 6.30 a.m. until 6 p.m., with a half-day on Saturdays. Sundays were also free, after they had been to church. He could remember when London was lit by gas-lamps and had horse-drawn cabs. It seemed an incredible link with the past and I spent quite a few of my working hours listening to his stories.

Just as interesting to me was the career of his daughter Mary, who had read English at Oxford University and was then teaching at the University of Hong Kong as an assistant to Professor Edmund Blunden. Her father sent some of my poems to her which she showed to Blunden, and I was soon to correspond with this gentle poet of the English countryside who had survived the horrors of the trenches in the First World War. Because he was also one of the early and most dedicated of John Clare scholars it wasn't long before he was directing my attention to the Helpston poet's work. Edmund Blunden always wrote to me in exquisite handwriting on oriental postcards. He was one of those people who persuades one that *he* is grateful for the contact:

> A good postman today! He brought your letter and the sundries, of great interest. My best thanks. I like the poems and hope to say a word or two on them when we meet and luxuriate in our own style ...

We were to meet a few years later and share a few beers in the Blue Bell inn at Helpston. We also had our photograph taken in Clare's garden and, for a time, I must have brought that out from my wallet as often as Reg Oswin did his of the two princesses.

Knowing the Oswins opened up a few new horizons for me. Mary was passionate about the Brontës and the poetry of T.S. Eliot. Reg was a loyal conservative and churchwarden. His wife, Grace, was a staunch socialist and agnostic. Whenever there was an election their two front-room windows were postered in every pane with the publicity and propaganda of their respective parties. It was an early lesson for me on the compatibility of opposites. That all these experiences should be happening to me in the quiet backwaters of Whittlesey was a revelation.

It was whilst I was convalescing from an appendicitis operation that Reg Oswin offered to take me out for a drive and then to his house for tea. The suspension on his old car had known more responsive days and did little to smooth out the bumpy fen roads on which we travelled. Although I feared that my stitches would snap before they were ready to be removed I did not complain. I was grateful that I was being taken to parts of the Fens I had not known before – Holme Fen and the famous iron post which had recorded the shrinking of the land since Whittlesea Mere was drained in 1851. I was struck too by the colour and richness of the soil which was as black as liquorice.

If I remember correctly, Reg, as a southerner, did not like the Fens all that much, or the people, whom he found rather dull and uncultured. But he was not aloof, or detached from them. He did enjoy his visits to the pub and occasionally joined in a game of darts. He also appreciated our sunsets and often walked out into Conington Fen to watch what he called 'an exhibition of abstract art' displayed on the sky beyond the busy A1. It was he who persuaded me to concentrate my thoughts on the local landscape rather than to imitate those poets writing about Wales or Gloucestershire. Apart from the newly acquired poems of John Clare, the only other poets I read at that time were Dylan Thomas and Laurie Lee. When my first slim collection of verse *A Year to Come* was published in 1954, Reg took me round to a nearby pub for a couple of pints and made me read some of the poems aloud to him. I felt timidly Bohemian among the bemused customers, most of whom knew me for what I was. When I eventually met his daughter she whisked me off to London to see an Ingmar Bergman film and then to a coffee-house in Covent Garden. Like Clare, I felt that I had been pulled up by the roots and exported to another world.

And what has all this got to do with sunsets? Well, sunset-watching is a waiting-game. It can take anything from five minutes to half-an-hour to get a result. And, while you wait, you get to thinking about all kinds of things. So, as I was in the mood for a sunset, I went out to Holme and Conington Fen, knowing that it would be a good place to wait should all the necessary conditions come together at the right moment to oblige. They didn't. That was at least one sunset a poet couldn't spoil. Instead I sat and thought about the people I had once known there, people who were different and whom I admired for their independent and eccentric freedom.

However, I did not give up my quest for a sunset and had better luck the following evening when I drove along Glassmoor Bank towards Chapel Bridge. There I was able to park the car and look back down the long straight drain known as Bevil's Leam. Again, as I waited, I was able to think of some of the people I had once met who worked on the surrounding farms – the farm foreman who would not believe that men had landed on the moon; the farmer who claimed that his dog could crack a coconut in its jaws more easily than most dogs could break a walnut; the woman who, after bearing fourteen children, said it was time to get back to work. By the time I had amused myself with those recollections the sun was already mixing a palette of fiery colours with which to end the day. Soon it reached its awesome climax, casting a dye of pink, amber and red across the whole sky so that the higher layers of cloud above me echoed the same tones, like a descant to the main theme. This was no minor farewell on the western horizon. It covered two-thirds of the earth. Had my friends been with me, they would have been impressed.

It is only now, years later, that I can see how these casual, or predestined encounters had an effect on my life. Many of the people who came to mind during the writing of this chapter have either died or left the area. But for a few moments the Fens held them, like a bright colour in the sky and, because of that, the world was changed in some small way even if they did not know it. The extraordinary thing to me now is that I can see how they all fit into a pattern, random shapes gathered into a whole; a puzzle nearly solved. A reason for gratitude.

But before concluding this subject of sunsets and their effect on me, it is only proper that I should concede that not everyone sees them as a cause for celebration. Dramatic though they sometimes are, they often speak for others, not of a brief creation of beauty but as a slow symbol of death, the last flicker before darkness and night. The poet Robert Browning reminds us that:

Just when we are safest, there's a sunset touch,
A fancy from a flower-bell, someone's death ...

Shakespeare, too, used sunsets as a picture of old age:

In me thou see'st the twilight of such day
As after sunset fadeth in the west;
Which by and by black night doth take away,
Death's second self, that seals up all in rest ...

However, it would still be wrong to end this chapter on such a mournful and pessimistic note. After all, it is not the sun that dies, or sinks, or fades away. Although it is consuming its own energy at a rate of several million tons a day it is still, as far as we are concerned, constant and will rise again the following day. Won't it?

17 'And I Saw a New Heaven and a New Earth'

Forgive me for taking on the mantle of St John the Divine, just for a moment, but I could find no better title for this chapter than those words which he was to use in the Book of Revelation. Although my vision may not quite have matched his I still felt, as I approached the final pages of my book, that I too had been blessed with revelations undreamt of when I began, and that the seal was about to be placed on what I had subsequently written.

The year had already given me many memorable days in the Fens and the last few weeks were not to be any the less full of surprise as well as delight. I had been to previously unknown parts of the Fens and yet more were still to be shown to me.

It had not been my intention to continue these celebrations into the winter months for I had covered that season more than any other in my earlier books. But one coincidence followed another and, by the time I caught up with the consequences, December was upon me. Again, the beginnings of this chapter go back to something that happened many years ago, nearly thirty if my calculations are correct. I was at the time compiling a series of programmes about the countryside for BBC Schools broadcasts and had been asked to go out into the Fens with a tape-recorder to interview anyone who could give the young listeners – many of them city-dwellers – some idea of what it was like to live 'in the country', especially in the wintertime.

One of the people I interviewed was Mr Ted Easton who, among many other occupations, was a mole-catcher employed by the drainage board to keep the river-banks free of moles – those little destroyers whose colonies could riddle the bank with their burrows and consequently weaken the defences against possible floods. Ted was also an expert catcher of eels, maker of eel-nets and a weaver of baskets, a man who had a lifetime's experience in country matters and a love of wild-life – including moles.

The day I was out with him he showed me where and how he planted the traps, explained why his narrow spade was called a spud – a word I had only come across before in the poetry of John Clare, and why he hung the caught moles on a wire fence a few days later. It was a cold day and the wind hissed and whistled into the microphone. I also had an unexpected over-load on the recorder as Ted shouted to his dog 'Spider' to 'come back you ...' The rest of the sentence had to be edited out because it was for a school's programme. But the mole-catcher gave me the dream of an interview and I knew that I had been in the company of a real fenman.

I did not expect to meet him again, nor, as the years passed, to find him coming back into my writing, as much as I would have relished it. It was not until a couple of years ago, when I was in the company of a young farmer who had married a friend of ours, that the coincidence occurred. 'I think you knew my grandfather,' he said. Did I? He then told me that his grandfather was Ted Easton. And that was not the only coincidence for I soon learned that Roger, the grandson, was now farming land in Holme Fen that had belonged to another old friend, Eric Slote, who had died the previous year. I had written about Eric in my book *Spirit of the Fens* and often went to see him in his new bungalow. I certainly did not expect to be visiting his farms again.

Later that day Roger was to provide the missing link by taking me to meet his father, Gordon Easton. So, from a chance meeting with a mole-catcher thirty years ago, I found myself in 1995 setting out early one winter morning to visit his grandson at Wype Doles Farm, Angle Bridge. A sharp frost overnight had covered every bush, hedge and tree with glittering silver. The air itself had a frosted, mother-of-pearl look about it, shot as it was with flashes of amber and blue as the rising sun slowly heaved itself over the hard horizon. The white branches then had touches of gold-leaf and the ice on the river appeared to be glowing with its own inner fire. It was a winter world of legends and folk-tales. I would not have been surprised to see mythical creatures leaping across the dykes or a Walt Disney castle suddenly appearing in the distance.

The roads were still icy and so I took care, knowing that the person I was going to see had himself recently been presented with a bravery award by the Royal Humane Society for helping to save a woman's life after she had plunged off the road in her car into a nearby dyke of freezing water. A moment later she would have been dead.

Having reached Angle Bridge safely I turned down the private road by the river and eventually found Roger's house. And this is where I must say something about the unusual name of his farm – Wype Doles. There are many strange place-names in the Fens and they do not always mean what they imply. Take Honey Hill near Chatteris, for instance. This has nothing to do with bees, or honey, but is named after Bishop Huna who officiated at the burial of St Etheldreda in Ely. Afterwards he retired and went to live on a remote island which became known as Huna's Hill; then, by the corruption of time, as Honey Hill.

There are several areas in the Fens with the word Doles in their name. Dole was an Old English word meaning a strip of land, especially of common meadow, granted annually to graziers or drovers. Some of this land provided revenue for some very different causes. Fees from Cantors' Doles once helped to pay the lay-clerks' salaries at Ely Cathedral. But what about Wype Doles? Wype is an old fenland word for lapwing, or peewit. I am therefore persuaded that Wype Doles means a meadow where flocks of lapwings gathered for the winter. The origin of the word lapwing also gives us some idea of why we call the peewit by that more apt name. In Old English it was spelt *leapewince*, then in Middle English it became *lappewinke*, which described its flight as it leapt and tumbled in the air with the coquettish movement of a winking eye. Other explanations have been offered but I still prefer to think of Wype Doles as lapwing pastures, i.e. their share of the country. That did not mean they were spared the risk of being hunted. Lapwings, like skylarks, were once snared in their thousands and sent to London to become delicacies in restaurants and at banquets.

After showing me round some of his many barns, with their expensive and sophisticated machinery that had reduced twelve men's labour to one, we set off to look at some of the two thousand acres that he and his father farmed.

The land was still sprinkled with salt-white frost, the water in the dykes frozen solid. Telegraph wires, coated with ice, hung with all the glitter of necklaces from pole to pole. Close by a large heron rose from the dykeside, a grey phoenix rising from the white ash of the ancient reeds. 'It's good to know that the heron population is increasing in the Fens, isn't it,' said Roger, who is enthusiastic about the preservation of the countryside and its wild life, helping, like Alwyn Johnson, to keep a count of all the birds that use the Fens.

Again, I found myself travelling over land on which I had never set foot before, even though it was only a few miles from where I was born. It was like exploring a previously undiscovered country full of strange sights and impressions.

Then we arrived at Glassmoor Bank and I knew where I was. We were on our way to Holme Fen, which was familiar territory but then made more interesting because I was in the company of a man who could take me to places I would not dream of going, down deep-rutted droves and into fields marked 'strictly private'. There I was to see some of the stacked bog-oaks which Roger had pulled out of his land that summer. They stood like black crumbling pyramids beside the banks of Bevil's Leam, the huge bones of a forgotten age, finally revealed by the shrinking soil and the powerful ploughshare – which did not always win. Roger agreed with me that the theory of these massive tree trunks 'floating' to the surface was not acceptable. It was the gradual lowering of the land that was now exposing them. Their like would never be seen again for they were part of the past that could not be repeated in our lifetime.

As we left this monument to an earlier history we disturbed a Chinese miniature deer that went leaping off to some nearby cover. At the end of the field we crossed the road to check on yet another barn stacked to the roof with potatoes, and a sparrow hawk sat on the corner of the building, watching us with great interest.

I asked Roger which, out of all his crops, were the ones which gave him greatest satisfaction. 'Potatoes,' he said.

'They're the most satisfying, from putting in the seed to lifting and riddling. You can see the results of your labours.' We then talked about wheat and how farmers were coping with the problem of no longer being allowed to burn corn-stubble. 'It was the best thing that ever happened. Once we'd learnt how to adjust our machines and to cope it soon made sense. It's better for the land to plough the stubble back in, much better than burning, especially on our peat fields which are very combustible.'

I felt we were then bouncing over bumpier ground that was higher than the rest. 'They're the suet Hills,' said Roger. Hills? thought I! More like suet dumplings. I looked at my Ordnance Survey map and saw that they were marked as ancient tumuli. So who had been there before us? There were no significant mounds but, as we drove on, I saw that we were actually going downhill to the next field, which belonged to the London Brick Company. Beneath that land still lay a great depth of valuable clay, a deposit from the Jurassic sea which formed the blue-grey substance from which modern man learnt to make bricks. One day that clay will be excavated, and what secrets will be revealed then? In the past similar diggings have uncovered complete skeletons of prehistoric animals between 150 million and 500 million years old. It helps to put life into perspective. From Fields End Bridge we made our way to Whittlesey and then Coates, where I was to meet Roger's father, Gordon Easton.

Naturally it wasn't long before we were talking about *his* father, the mole-catcher, and of those times when life was much harder for people.

I can remember my Dad telling me that one year, when he was employed spreading dyke-earth for five shillings a week, the winter was that hard they couldn't do any work, so there wasn't any money coming in either. They couldn't even afford anything for a proper Christmas dinner. Their next-door neighbours were in the same boat. So my father took his gun and his last two cartridges and went out to see what he could find in the fields. He came back a bit later with a hare, which they split down the middle, one half to each family, so that they got a Christmas dinner of sorts after all.

The Eastons then lived out at Thorney Dyke and had to

get their water from the river opposite. That was Gordon's job before he went off to school each morning. He showed me the yoke he used to use, one pail each side, and told me how they had to eke out the water, especially in dry weather. 'I think there's been more changes in my lifetime than there was in the past 500 years.'

I also learned that Gordon had many hobbies, including collecting old farm implements, tools, whips, machinery and wagons. I asked him how he managed to find all those things. 'I mooch about a bit,' which was the kind of fulsome answer I would have expected from a fenman. But his greatest passion was undoubtedly reserved for his masterpieces, some beautiful and priceless gypsy caravans which he was in the process of restoring, with the help of one or two gypsy friends who were making sure that everything down to the smallest detail was authentic. 'Did you know,' he asked, 'that every true and genuine gypsy caravan must have its own angel?' He showed me the ones he had had made to adorn his. 'They're very religious people, gypsies – and I mean the real Romanys.' I was overwhelmed by the craftsmanship and artistry that went into all the fittings and decorations, each piece steeped in tradition, each section being made of a certain wood, each scroll painted a special colour, the stove enamelled and the windows patterned with the same symbols that gypsies had used for centuries.

I was then taken to see a barn full of old farm wagons, some nineteenth century, carefully restored and now full of ghosts, hauntings of harvest scenes that would never grace the land again. I asked Gordon if such heavy wagons would have been pulled by Shire horses. 'No. That's a myth really,' he replied. 'They wouldn't have used Shires in the Fens because their legs were too hairy and would have got all drabbled with mud. They would have gone for something like Percherons, or Suffolks.'

It was getting close to lunchtime and I was taken out to the Oliver Twist pub at Guyhirn where a juicy steak-and-mushroom pie seemed appropriate fare for such a cold day. There was a generous and welcoming coal fire blazing in the grate and we chose a table close to it. Then, more memories, more anecdotes, more char- acters. Some of them I had known. Most I had heard about. But there was (and still is) always something more worth hearing about them. One character, well-known in the Whittlesey area for uttering sentences that often came out backwards, was having a new handle fitted to the door of his wooden railway-carriage where he and his family lived. When asked by the workman on which side of the door the handle should be fixed, he said 'Put it on the inside, bor. We goo out more than we come in.'

I then asked to hear more of the Eastons' own family history. What had been the secret of their success? 'We always made a point of ploughing any profit we made back into the land, even if it meant going without ourselves,' said Gordon.

> There were some hard times in the beginning, I can tell you. At the end of the week we probably had enough to pay the wages of the men and women who worked for us but frequently had nothing left for ourselves. Sometimes I used to go out to do a bit of shooting to see if I could get a few brace of pheasants to sell. We also kept pigs and chickens, so we could always feed ourselves. That's how it was. A step at a time. Never over-reaching, but never missing an opportunity either. It was hard work and a never-give-up attitude that kept us going. And to think when I were a lad I nearly became apprenticed to a barber!

I noticed his private smile.

We had travelled quite a few miles in the course of the day but I had still not seen half of the land now farmed by the Eastons. As we drove back to Coates a freezing mist hovered over Kingsland Fen. It was like a mysterious sea slowly flowing in without actually touching the land beneath, or ever reaching the shore.

Also across the surrounding fields lay the course of the Roman road from Barnack, via Peterborough, Whittlesey, Eldernell, to March and beyond. How many such brilliant winter days would those legions have known? Efficient as the Romans were they could not, I'm sure, have experienced the pleasure I had of admiring a landscape now tamed and skilfully farmed by men like the Eastons, winning, as they have, many trophies for 'the best kept farm'.

There were still more things to see and much more to talk about, but Roger was anxious that I should be starting my way home before the mist became a fog. We returned

to Wype Doles, to the dogs and the donkeys, and I looked
again over that white, silent and impressive world that
was this man's life. 'You couldn't have been anything
other than what you are, could you Roger?' He looked at
me as if I had uttered some awful blasphemy, then said,
'No. I'm a very happy man.'

I drove off towards the bright-red opulent sun. And, as
if I needed a perfect ending to such a day, I was delighted
to find that the Whittlesey Washlands were flooded *and*
frozen, with about fifty people skating in the hazy middle
distance. Bruegel would have loved it. The low sun was
reflected in the ice. The skaters – partly silhouetted –
glided backwards and forwards in a timeless pattern that
man had been making in the Fens since skates were
invented. It was the final touch, a valediction, a vision as
inspiring as anything seen by any prophet or evangelist.
This was man and nature working together in complete
harmony, for pleasure.

This was the world that satisfied most, whatever the
season.

18   In Years to Come

During this pleasant task of being a self-appointed
chronicler of life in the Fens I like to believe that I have
picked up a few things that might otherwise have been
lost, that I have heard echoes in the wind strumming some
ancient truths on the web of our history; a web which, like
an Aeolian harp, has vibrated with the music for which
there are no words, nor ever will be now.

Despite this enjoyable commitment there are still times
when I find it difficult to explain to strangers why the
flatness of this land repeatedly wins over the beauty of
say, the Swiss Alps or the golden sun-parched antiquity of
Greece; why a wet day on the Welney Washlands can be
as memorable as a long drive through the baked
mountains of Spain or the aloof grandeur of the Canadian
Rockies. But that is how it is. I have tried them all, been
impressed by them all, and will go back to some of them
again. But I still have to return to the inevitable landscape
of the Fens to refresh the springs of my own existence and
the main source of my creativity whilst it lasts. It clearly
has something to do with more than picturesque scenery.
Just as human love goes beyond physical beauty, so one's
love for a place goes deeper than what is usually enjoyed
for mere pleasure, or simply out of curiosity. One knows
instinctively where one belongs and for what reason.
There is no pretence. No need to lie about it, or to impress.
The giving and the receiving are the same. It's as natural
as a marriage. Questions do not always have to be
answered even if they are asked. There is an unspoken
understanding. A landscape is a condition of the spirit
which knows both longing and satisfaction.

When I take visitors out into the Fens they often
comment on how featureless to their eyes are the scenes

which so excite me. John Clare had a similar problem when his London publisher, John Taylor, came up to visit him in Helpston. Clare took him for a walk as far as Barnack, pointing out several of the places that had inspired so many of his poems, but Taylor confessed later that one needed the imaginative eye of a poet to see any beauty in what appeared to him to be 'very ordinary scenery indeed'. And that was about an area which, by comparison with the lower Fens, most people would consider modestly attractive, stretching as it does along the limestone ridge from Stamford into Northamptonshire. Clare was disappointed that his publisher had failed to appreciate the natural world which meant so much to him and to which he had to return if he was to continue writing the kind of poetry that only he could write – poetry which was also to become history.

In the same way I know that I have to keep in touch with the landscape of my nurturing because memory deceives and little that we see through the eyes of maturity can ever be quite as untarnished, or as lovely, as when it was first seen through the eyes of innocence. Some may well say that this is taking refuge in an unreal world, that we cannot go back however hard we try because the past is irretrievably gone. 'Years are', as the poet R.S. Thomas wrote, 'miles to be/travelled in memory/only ...'

This is probably true if we exist only within our concept of time. The question is when does reality take over? And where? Does it come sooner to those who leave home early in life, never to return? Or does it come to those who never leave home at all and have no other yard-stick by which to judge their beliefs or existence? As I said in my introduction, sometimes we need to be exiled in order to find out who we are and where we belong. Distance is sometimes necessary if we are to value what was once taken for granted. Did we get it wrong? Did we only imagine a world that never existed in the first place – a world of make-believe to disguise reality? Or are we now simply feeling the longings of those who, many generations ago, put down their roots into a new land and made it home? It is all too easy to romanticize. Easier still to go on posing questions to which there are no satisfactory answers. Yes, as Robert Browning reminded us, 'A man's reach should exceed his grasp,/Or what is heaven for?'

As I looked again over the vast expanse of land that had almost resigned itself to winter I knew that one answer would always be the same for me, even if I could not explain it adequately to anyone else. It is like being aware of a certain truth. The generous year was ending. A cold light filled the sky. Its nakedness was reflected in the river below. Sky and water – each one a mirror echoing the other; echoing also the past as well as the present. The broad sheet of water was motionless, the sky a silver screen on which memory could project any episode which came to mind and give it life. All I had to do was to stand and watch.

There was the child I used to be, walking along the field's edge, puffing at dandelion clocks to tell some mythical time, or picking simple flowers. He was not conscious then of what that great space around him was doing to his imagination, day by day. There too were the tall reed-mace as tempting as dark chocolate, and there a rash of poppies which he was not allowed to pick because superstition had it that if he did he would wet the bed that night. The icy bleakness of the sky had given way to a cornflower-blue and I watched that child throwing stones into the water, or learning how to rub an ear of wheat in

Sky and water – each one a mirror

his hands to taste the new corn of that summer. It was like being reminded of some ancient ceremony.

Slowly, frame by frame I saw a score of summers pass in coloured random. I did not choose them. They came like raffled reminders out of a hat – the recreation-ground with its swings and roundabout, its sand-pit and water fountain, from which that boy always had to drink. There were those days too when he stood outside the blacksmith's forge, mesmerized by the bellows breathing life into a sleeping fire, blinking as the sparks suddenly flew from the red-hot iron that was being beaten into a shoe for the horse waiting in the paddock opposite. The ring of the rhythmic hammer-blows echoed back over the years. And then there were those sultry afternoons of liquorice shoe-laces and sherbet from the little sweet-shop in Station Road, of ice-creams and picnics – simple affairs with no more than a soft-cheese sandwich and a slice of cake, but how much better they tasted when eaten by the riverside than in the stuffy room at home where all the usual meals were taken.

Sky and water ... Nature's hall of mirrors through which I had been lured to glimpse again those moments which had gone into the making of the whole. There was the classroom at the Infants' School in Broad Street and the young teacher (who was later to become Mrs Merritt mentioned in Chapter 3), patiently teaching me to count with yellow shells. The jar of sticky chestnut buds on which her skirt got caught was still there. So too were the high Victorian windows out of which I daily stared, longing for freedom. It was more than sky and water, earth and grass. Each remembered image became a glimpse of that child in paradise. The air smelt good, more pure and clean than now. That boy walked in a state of wonder, surrounded by creation. Nothing was ordinary. 'All appeared new and strange ... inexpressibly rare and delightful and beautiful.' Traherne's words of 300 years ago had not faded.

Later reminders showed how the boy had grown, cycling deeper into that world than he had ever been before. Wonder had now added to it a sense of adventure. He watched the corn being reaped, smelt the cart-loads of newly pulled peas as they went down the street; saw the potatoes lifted like gold coins out of the ancient earth;

each day counted the skylarks above his head; observed the sun slowly setting beyond the smoking brickyard chimneys.

How did he, or I, fit into that world? I realized now that for most of that time I had been blind to what was happening to me and had no idea until I was well into my twenties that I would ever want to write about that world. I had no literary ambitions or talent then. It had simply been a private, personal affair which I had never considered sharing with others. From when I was about ten years old I had always gone out into the Fens alone. I loved solitude and quietness. It was not until I started writing that I began to think that others might be persuaded to appreciate the beauty I believed was there. The trouble with voices from the past is that they are inevitably receding as one gets older, and the pictures fade. This is one reason why I have decided to put down what I can remember and have gleaned what I can from the memories of others.

I would like to think that in my celebration of this withdrawn and unromantic country we call the Fens, I have not been sentimental at the expense of accuracy, that I have not blinded the unconverted with false images, or have over-reached myself. There are, I am sure, still many things out there to grasp, but not yet. Tomorrow will find its own legends, its own heroes and characters to perpetuate the folklore of a region of Britain that it would be unwise to ignore completely. As I hope I have shown, there is always something else to learn, some new place to discover.

Several times during the preceding chapters I have referred to the changes that have taken place in the Fens during the last fifty or sixty years, changes that are obvious and not necessarily unique to this part of England. Most rural areas have been affected by change of one sort or another. But, living in a place for the greater part of one's life, it is possible to become oblivious to the subtler transformation going on, to the disappearance of customs and the shift of interests. As we have seen, many of the daily jobs that were once associated with the Fens have already disappeared – beet-hoers, potato-pickers and, to some extent, celery-prickers. I shall no longer be able to write about the people who once did that kind of work:

For three days those few women
Have hoed a long field of sugar-beet,
Their blue and red cardigans
Reduced to the size of cornflower or poppy.

They have chopped at the weeds
With a precision older than clockwork.
Their arms have a rhythm
That goes back almost to Adam ...

nor shall I be able to say of the celery-prickers.

You say too easily
There's virtue living near the soil.
Those women crawling on all-fours
Pricking out celery-plants would not agree.

For them there is no comfort in a cold east wind
Whipping their broad behinds all day.
Even the canvas screens around each bed
Cannot protect them from the black wet earth ...

The same could be said about horse-keepers and thackers – those skilled men of the land who could build and top a stack as though it were architect designed, stacks that would not lurch or topple in the wind. Gone too are the potato-clamps – those long heaps or 'graves' of potatoes that were strawed and packed down on the headlands until the market was ready for them and the riddling began. Now they are stored in large temperature-controlled barns, such as those used by Roger Easton. Once upon a time they decorated the winter landscape like ancient burial mounds. Now they have taken their place in the pages of history, along with reap-hooks, binders and working-horses. So rapid have been these changes that I still find it hard to believe that within this century woad was being grown in the Fens. The last working woad-mill at Parson Drove was not demolished until 1914. I don't suppose the crop could complain that its own long history had come to an end for it began before the early Britons wore its blue dye to scare off the Romans, not very successfully.

Which of today's crops will go the same way? Oil-seed rape, or linseed? Celery or oats? When I asked one young farmer how he saw the future of farming in the Fens, and what changes there would be, he said:

Computers! Everything will be done by computers. It's already started. We shall simply send out programmed machines into the fields to do the work for us. Tractors will be driven by remote control. Ploughs will be operated by a button pressed in the office. White coats will take the place of wellies and your traditional farm-worker will be a thing of the past. You need to have a degree or two now as it is.

And, I enquired tentatively, some of the fields will disappear too? 'They're bound to. So I should make the most of the Fens while you can. The developers are waiting.' Or the sea, I said. 'Ah! If that happens, which it could, we shall all have to think again. Nature may well have the last laugh.' It reminded me of Gordon Easton's concern that most of the drainage pumps in the Fens were now driven by electricity, which is one of the first sources of energy we lose in times of floods or blizzards. It only needs one or two major power-lines to be brought down and the pumps which are there to protect us are made as helpless as windmills without wind.

It was put to me on more than one occasion during the year that there was no purpose in lamenting the passing of those historic scenes and customs of which I was writing. Maybe not, and I am sufficiently informed to know that with their demise went not only hard manual labour but illness, despair and injustice. Medical care was expensive, employers often fickle and unsentimental. A good boss and a good worker were a happy combination perpetuated through several generations. A family that could keep itself reasonably healthy with its home-grown produce and home-cures, and retain a regular job, considered itself fortunate. When I look at some of the derelict cottages left scattered in the Fens today, their backs broken with subsidence, their gardens now full of nettles and the outdoor lavatories as guilty as ruined confessionals, I can fully understand that the word 'heaven' was not one which those people would have used to describe their meagre existence.

What has also disappeared are some of the less attractive customs, such as lark-snaring, badger-hunting and cock-fighting. There are not that many skylarks left to snare now but it is occasionally whispered in my ear that cock-fighting still goes on secretly in the remote barns of the Fens and weekend hare-coursing still persists. It is also true to say that many of those unwelcome activities are pursued today by people from the towns, often newcomers who believe that blood-sports are an essential part of the 'country life'. Such a natural state of existence is now something of a myth. Country life, as I have seen it day by day, is simply getting on with surviving in a world that is threatened, like anywhere else. The world is now a small place. Any part of it can be brought into our homes at will. The external influences are very persuasive. The retreat is losing ground. Some people will adapt, others take refuge in their memories of what life was like when they were more free to enjoy its simple and personal benefits. For a man born before the first tractor chugged its way into the Fens it is difficult to believe that it is now possible to explore the outer regions of space. But such men still exist and wonder if we're sane.

In trying to bring together all the intricate strands of fenland life I find myself saying again that, in the end, each landscape, each place, is essentially a personal one and only we can say why it means as much to us as it does. It is like putting on a favourite coat that others may think is getting a little too worn, or is out of date. But if it fits, if it is still comfortable, if it keeps one warm, why discard it? If someone else wishes to borrow it occasionally then we should feel honoured.

Much of the love I feel for the Fens today is, of course, rooted in the Fens of yesterday because those experiences helped to make me what I am. But I could not have enjoyed the place more than I did during the writing of this book. As I look back over that year, I know that I savoured some of the most satisfying hours that I have ever spent in the Fens and, in years to come, will surely bore my few surviving friends with recollections of 'the finest wheat fields I ever saw' or 'the bluest skies you could ever wish for' or 'I can remember some of the hottest days of the century when ...' And even if I do not have an audience to share such memories with I shall be able to recall the blissful times I spent out at Guy's Head and Christchurch, at Parson Drove and Gedney, and I shall think of those pleasant hours I spent with such friendly people as Constance and Tom Crouch, Alwyn Johnson, Gordon and Roger Easton, and I shall probably mutter to myself, 'we don't have men and women like that any more.'

It occurs to me now that most of what I had been writing about during that year would, indeed, soon be in the last century, that by the time these words appear in print there will be just over three years to go before the millennium. It tempts me to believe that there could be some historical significance to what I have been trying to say, that my efforts in aiming to preserve a little of what has been happening in the Fens during the past hundred years, has been justified. I hope so for the sake of all the good Fen people I have known.

And so, like all celebrations, these pages must come to an end. It was appropriate that the winter's first fall of snow should have arrived to put its own seal on the year when it did. The fields, which had displayed so many vibrant colours in the summer and autumn, were suddenly white, the land a blank page on which no word had yet been written. It was as if we were being invited to make a new beginning, to plant the next footprints upon the earth with a greater sense of adventure, to touch the frozen web that was now waiting for its silent music to be heard.

If time, space, history and life all move in circles, then I can do no better than to return to the words of Elizabeth Barrett Browning with which I prefaced Part 1 of this volume:

> ... only he who sees, takes off his shoes;
> The rest sit round and pluck blackberries.

It is not my intention to sit around doing that and hopefully I shall be off in a few months time in search of other aspects of this heaven on earth. It may be the only one I shall inherit.

Index